LET IT GO

LET IT GO

• • •

A True Story of Tragedy and Forgiveness

CHRIS WILLIAMS

SHADOW
MOUNTAIN

Photos courtesy of the Chris Williams family: pages vi, 11, 45, 56, 90, 105, 128, 142, 146, 148.

Photos courtesy of *Deseret News*: page 4 (Tom Smart), page 26 (Mike Terry), page 50 (Jeffrey D. Allred), page 61 (August Miller), page 79, page 86 (Scott G. Winterton), page 124 (Kristy Nichols). Used by permission.

Photo on page 140 © Intellectual Reserve, Inc. Used by permission.

Visit us at ShadowMountain.com

Library of Congress Cataloging-in-Publication Data

Williams, Chris (Chris Stuart), author.
  Let it go / Chris Williams.
    pages cm
  Summary: "When his wife and two of his children were killed in a drunk-driving accident, Chris Williams made the most important decision of his life"—Provided by publisher.
  ISBN 978-1-60907-127-1 (hardbound : alk. paper)
  1. Williams, Chris (Chris Stuart) 2. Mormons—Biography. 3. Bereavement—Religious aspects—The Church of Jesus Christ of Latter-day Saints. I. Title.
  BX8695.W5445A3 2012
  248.8'66—dc23   2012013801

Printed in the United States of America
Publishers Printing

10 9 8 7 6 5 4 3 2 1

To Michelle, Benjamin, and Anna Williams

The Williams family, Christmas Eve 2006
Front (left to right): Anna, Michelle, Chris, Sam
Back: Ben, Michael

● ● ●

Contents

CONTENTS

• • •

Introduction

"I am not that smart or emotionally strong," I said as I moved closer to emphasize that point. "I couldn't have done it on my own." I paused, trying to restrain my emotions as I struggled to revisit that tragic night when the car I was driving was hit by a drunk teenage driver, killing my wife, who was five months pregnant, and two of our four children.

Throughout my lunch with this young couple, Tyler and Emily,* we conversed as if we had known one another for years, with each of us sharing intimate details of the trials we were enduring. Our differing journeys had led us to this sharing of experiences of grief and self-reflection, yet this was the first time we had ever met. They had recently lost a child in a terrible accident and were struggling to forgive themselves and those who were involved. A mutual friend had suggested that it might be helpful if we met, if for no other reason than for them to know they weren't alone on their grief-filled journey.

*Names of couple have been changed.

1

As we visited, we shared our thoughts about the horrible feelings a tragedy or trial can produce in our lives and about the perceived loss of control over our circumstances. We pondered together each of our prior expectations for the future, and how everything now was so very different, and not by our choice. We commiserated about how the only thing that is truly ours—our will—felt as if it too was being compromised or taken from us in some way.

Tyler had been very direct. He wanted to know how I had forgiven the driver immediately after the crash, asking me how I was able to "keep moving forward rather than go through months or years of anguish struggling to let it go?" They both spoke of being emotionally and physically drained as a result of their tragedy. They were tired of "feeling stuck" and earnestly wanted to find peace.

"I am a quick study when properly motivated," I said. "But, unfortunately, I've found that whatever knowledge I thought I had gained in those cram sessions usually didn't stick as well as something that was painfully pressed into my soul over a longer period of time.

"To make matters worse," I continued, "I am not a very patient person. I want answers and a resolution to my struggles before I'm prepared to comprehend the answer or fully appreciate the relief." Tyler nodded his head in acknowledgement, while Emily shared similar experiences of struggling with patience and perseverance, of desperately awaiting a release from the trial they were enduring.

As the conversation progressed, I became increasingly concerned that my attempts to provide the answers and comfort they sought were falling short. My suspicion was confirmed when, after talking together for almost an hour, Tyler interrupted my explanation of what I had gained from the forgiveness by saying, "I can see how it's possible to forgive and heal, and even why it's necessary to do so—I get that—but I still don't understand how *you* were able to let it go and move forward so immediately, right after the crash." He didn't want textbook admonitions regarding the virtues of forgiveness, or a reminder that it was ultimately the right thing to do for him or his wife or anyone else who has been hurt. He was willing to be completely open and wanted me to do the same. He hoped to peer deeper into my soul to tap the strength he thought I had found—he wanted a much more personal and unfiltered view into my life than I had yet been willing to provide. He wanted to pierce the public façade we all put up when we interact with one another and, by so doing, see me as I really was.

I suddenly felt very vulnerable and much more exposed in their presence. I knew I had to go back to that horrible, excruciating moment in the car just prior to the decision and commitment I made to let it go. I didn't know where to start. I struggled to preface that terrible refining experience by reviewing my life prior to the crash. I expressed my hopes that I had tried to live so that I could be thought of and described as one who tried to cultivate a peaceable walk among the children of men in his life, one who tried to "do unto others" as I would have them do to me. As I continued, images of the crash began to flash in my mind, and I was now acutely aware and careful of what I was saying, as if I were on trial, justifying my life before them. My explanations started sounding hollow as I began, in my mind's eye, to envision the exterior of our mangled car that had just been hit, and what I must have looked like after the impact—seated inside the car, in shock and desperately trying to process what was happening.

My life's justification was now sounding increasingly

Chris at the 20th East underpass, February 2008

desperate. I stopped speaking. I could now clearly see myself seated in the car after the impact, so helpless, so very helpless. I couldn't speak as the flood of emotions choked my ability to continue. My eyes were directed at the table between us, but I was unable to see anything but the image of a father whose life had just been shattered. Slowly I looked up. Tyler was leaning forward, his gaze fixed on my eyes, and Emily had begun to weep. I looked directly into his eyes so he could somehow see the scene I was observing in my mind, and I shared the first thing they needed to know about my reactions at the crash site: "I am nothing."

• • •

I

"O Be Wise"

I wish there were a way to convey in words the annoying
sound my old alarm clock made. I spent several days piecing together consonants and vowels to represent the most horrid, grating, angry electronic buzzing sound possible, but everything I
wrote ended up looking like some kind of inappropriate word.
I would set the alarm to sound promptly at 6:00 A.M., retiring
to bed with every intention of rising in the morning alert and
full of energy, only to be jolted awake by that hideous noise.
Irritated by the buzzing sound, I smacked at the alarm until the
noise stopped. Maybe I enjoyed that small victory at the start of
each day, exerting control over my little world and, as a reward,
receiving another five minutes of sleep. It was short-lived, however. After the five minutes passed, the alarm sounded again, the
snooze button was smacked, and I was still not terribly awake or
full of energy.

Throughout this high drama of man versus alarm, my
wife, Michelle, remained asleep by my side. She had a different

morning routine. When her alarm sounded (and it had a much nicer tone), she would arise, turn it off, and get out of bed. After nearly eighteen and a half years of marriage, she was reluctantly resigned to my snooze-button power struggle. If I had to be up at a certain hour, I would usually awake before the alarm sounded. Unfortunately for Michelle, I guess I had too many mornings when I just didn't need to be up that early.

She could get quite irritated when I chose to snooze rather than wake up, chiding my behavior by saying, "Why don't you just get up when the alarm goes off?" or "If you really intend to sleep to 6:30, why do you set the alarm for 6:00?" Sometimes I could see she was right, and I would apologize. But most of the time I felt quite justified staying in our comfy bed, especially on those mornings when I didn't need to be anywhere in particular.

As perplexed as she might have been about my tendencies, she wasn't above occasionally pushing me out of the bed, her feet extending quickly to my back, thrusting me through the sheets and onto the floor. But somewhere in our marriage she had come to a state of exasperated resignation, adapting to the noise to the point where she would just sleep through it all. I even tried putting that alarm across the room, forcing myself out of bed to hit the snooze button, but I would just turn around and plop back into bed until it went off again. It took Michelle a bit longer to tolerate that behavior as she didn't like the bed shaking when I jumped back in.

● ● ●

I met Michelle Dorny for the first time at Churchill Jr. High School in Salt Lake City, Utah. A straight-A student, active in sports and various activities, and upon reflection, one of the most beautiful girls in the school, Michelle was wonderful to be around. We were friends throughout high school, going on double dates together but never dating each other. I think that was fortunate. Perhaps dating her then would have ruined any chance with her in the future. I always felt that she was incredibly polished and refined while I, on the other hand, needed a bit more work.

After I graduated from high school, I wanted to serve a proselytizing and service mission for The Church of Jesus Christ of Latter-day Saints, and I was subsequently assigned to the Paraguay, Asunción mission, deep in the heart of South America. I give that little bit of geographical reference because when I received my assignment I had no idea exactly where Paraguay was. It probably took away from the anticipation and excitement of the moment when, after reading "You have been called to serve in the Paraguay, Asunción Mission," I then looked at my mom in bewilderment and asked, "Where's that?" Perhaps I should have balanced all the science classes I took in high school with at least one more geography class. Before I had even figured out on a map where Paraguay was, I was wondering if the country had been mistyped and I was really going to Parasite, Asunción. And yes, I contracted several while I was there, thank you very much! It was probably life's way of giving me a bit of payback for my flippant, lighthearted word association while we scrambled to find a map.

The geographical confusion aside, the time I spent in Paraguay was a wonderful way for me to realize that the world extended so much farther beyond the city limits where I was born and raised, and that I wasn't the center of the universe as I had sometimes supposed. The wonderful experiences I had working and serving in Paraguay, among a people that I came to love dearly, remain among the sweetest and most important memories of my life. I'm satisfied that there is no better place on earth where I could have served. I became better prepared for life and a bit more refined as well.

I had only been home from Paraguay a little over a month when I saw Michelle at a dance at the University of Utah. She too had changed since high school. She was more striking in appearance and even more captivating, beautiful, poised, and confident. I remember being filled with awe at first sight. When I asked if she would like to dance, I think she hesitated at first and maybe even looked around for a way out. With no other prospects in sight, she reluctantly agreed. I don't think I had the same awe-inspiring effect on her.

After that evening, I reflected over and over on the impression she had made on me. I couldn't figure out—given all the double dates we had been on—why I had never thought to ask her out in all the years we had been friends. *How could I have possibly overlooked her,* I wondered. Certain that she remembered how I used to be back in high school, I was reluctant to pick up the phone to ask her out. When I finally did muster up the nerve to call her, I bumblingly asked, "Would you think it weird if I asked you out on a date?" In hindsight, I think just asking that kind of a question was weird. I've often wondered why I didn't just ask her to go on a date with me. Probably because I knew then that I would one day be the kind of guy that sets an alarm so I can hit the snooze button and get out of bed five minutes later than I intended to. In retrospect, I can't believe she said yes. Maybe it was just curiosity, but she agreed to go out with me nonetheless.

Our first date was wonderful. We went to dinner and then ice skating with a group of my friends. I loved how I felt in her presence. After the evening was over, I couldn't wait until the next time I was with her. With each subsequent date, I was inspired to be a better person, embrace life more fully, and serve others—all was right with the world. I don't think that even the sight of a unicorn flying through the air trailing a rainbow would have made me more enchanted; it was simply unbelievable the effect Michelle had on me.

I, unfortunately, was not having the same effect on her initially. I have since had the opportunity to read her journal entries from that time, and they're humbling to me even now. They confirmed what I suspected, that I didn't exactly sweep her off of her feet. She still had feelings for someone else that she hoped would be resolved somehow, either by rekindling that relationship or by ending it once and for all. It took us three years of an on-again, off-again courtship to get to a point where she would even entertain the concept of marrying me.

I had always thought, rather romantically and perhaps naively, I guess, that it shouldn't be that much work to fall in love. That may indeed be how it happens for most, but looking back on those years, I now see how she wanted to be sure I could love and serve unconditionally. As frustrating as that courtship became at times, at least I knew what any commitment to Michelle would involve: I would need to "court" her for the rest of my life.

Michelle inspired me to learn how to love and serve each week better than I had the week before. At one point while we were dating, she had an assignment to serve at a local nursing home. Rather than just fulfill the weekly time commitment to serve, she "adopted" a woman who was suffering from the effects of multiple sclerosis, visiting her as often as she could each week. I was privileged to accompany her on a few of those visits. I marveled at how she ministered with charity, as if the woman were a dearly beloved relative. That woman's last few months on earth were undoubtedly enriched by her association with Michelle.

9

Throughout her life, Michelle continued to serve and love others, and over the years together I was certainly blessed with much of that service. As a result of the continued courtship for nearly twenty years of marriage, she became the entire focus of my love, devotion, and attention; my whole identity was tied so closely to hers and who she had become. That is certainly one of the many reasons it was so difficult to lose her so suddenly.

• • •

In June 1988, Michelle and I rode the Snowbird tram to the top of the resort. Surrounded by the beautiful Wasatch Mountains and overlooking the Salt Lake Valley, I proposed. We were married two months later on August 18 at 6:30 in the morning in the Salt Lake Temple. We chose to be married in this sacred House of God with the faith that our marriage union would remain throughout eternity, and not just until we were parted by death. I knew that without heavenly help I wouldn't succeed as a husband or a father, and I desired the protection and clarity that having heaven's blessings would bring a new family like ours. Marrying Michelle, and doing so with an eternal focus from the very start, is one of the smartest decisions I have ever made. I guess I had come a long way since my days in high school, and she saw the potential that I was on my way to becoming the man she wanted to be with eternally.

After the ceremony we were congratulated by friends and family as we made our way to the east side of the building for photos. As the photographer positioned us on the steps of the temple, we saw the sun emerge from behind the Wasatch Mountains. It was one of the most powerful sunrises I have ever experienced. The light was a brilliant white and so intense that I

Chris and Michelle on their wedding day, August 1988

struggled to smile, keep my eyes open, and look somewhat normal for the photos. While I tried to endure the discomfort, it occurred to me that the brilliance of the sunrise was a great metaphor for the bright future ahead for Michelle and me. Sure it was a little corny, but it made an impression on me. The photos that captured that special moment only show me squinting and grimacing like I had a terrible migraine. Michelle, however, looked poised, confident, and absolutely gorgeous. I always say that she was used to brilliant light as she had lived in it all her life.

• • •

A few months after the tragedy, I had to travel on business to San Francisco. One early morning I decided to go for a run along the bay. As I left my hotel, I ran down Market Street toward

11

the waterfront and then turned south toward Pac Bell Park. As I passed the Bay Bridge, the sun emerged from behind the hills on the other side of the bay, and I was suddenly greeted with the same brilliant white light that I had witnessed on our wedding day. As I shielded my eyes, straining to regain my sight, I felt impressed that there were indeed brighter days ahead for me and that in the resurrection I would have an even more brilliant, joyful, and powerful future with Michelle. Tears filled my eyes as I recalled that wonderful morning with her on the steps of the temple immediately following a ceremony that made it possible for us to be together forever, even if we were now temporarily separated by a thin veil of death. I expressed my gratitude in prayer for that symbolic and spiritual witness, which strengthened my assurance of a future day made possible because of my Savior, Jesus Christ.

● ● ●

A few years after Michelle and I were married, we had our first child, Michael. He was named after Michelle's oldest brother, who had died in a scuba diving accident when he was twenty-one. The tragedy had occurred on Michelle's thirteenth birthday. As I dated Michelle and became more familiar with the terrible accident involving her brother, I resolved that two things would never happen in our relationship. First, I would never try to scuba dive, and second, I would never, ever let anything happen to Michelle. Each year as her birthday rolled around, I saw how concerned she was for her mother and father who still grieved the passing of their son. Michelle would downplay her own birthday celebration knowing that it was such a sad anniversary date in their family, especially for her mother. Our Michael was truly a blessing to the entire family as he was the first grandchild of Michelle's parents. I've always hoped that it provided additional healing to them to once again hear the name Michael spoken frequently in their home.

Soon after Michael was born, we tried to have another child; however, that pregnancy ended in a miscarriage. It was the first of several that Michelle would suffer and endure in her life. Each was a sad and devastating loss for her. Through the trials she endured, she never gave up hope or the desire for more children, and that faith and perseverance was rewarded as we were blessed with the addition of Benjamin in 1995, Anna in 1997, and Samuel in 2000.

Even with four children, we still lived in what we had called our "starter home" that we purchased before Michael was born. It was a modest home in a wonderful neighborhood. As the years passed and our family grew, we became less interested in moving into something larger and more interested in being debt-free. Given all of the financial turmoil that we have experienced in recent time, I wish I could attribute our foresight to some economic genius on my part, but sadly this isn't the case.

I did learn some economic lessons the hard way. One instance stands out firmly in my mind. One would think I would have been mindful of the new economic demands that came with a mortgage and a new baby; however, shortly after purchasing our home and when Michael was still a baby, I took the liberty one day to pay for a fast-food value meal with a check, written against an account that I had unknowingly spent down to zero. When I received the overdraft and returned-check fee notices, my four-dollar "value meal" actually cost about twenty-four dollars. When Michelle and I were balancing the checkbook and that little tidbit of joy came to light, I can't say I was too surprised to suddenly see the checkbook hurled at my face in frustration. Although I have since maintained, and still do to this day, that it was one of the tastiest burgers I have ever eaten—well worth the twenty-four dollars it cost—I still expect something to be hurled at my head when I finish making that claim.

We laughed about that experience many times, but Michelle wisely turned that overpriced value meal into a very valuable lesson on being unified in all things, especially finances. When we were counseled early in our marriage to get out of debt, Michelle and I committed to follow that counsel and pay off all our debts before considering moving anywhere else. Notwithstanding my initial financial ineptness, that unity working toward a common goal was rewarded. Ten years after buying our home, we were able to pay it off, along with every other debt, and we still had some money set aside for an emergency. The feeling of freedom from debt that we experienced was great, but it felt even more wonderful being united as a couple in our financial resolutions. I will always be incredibly grateful for the opportunity to work unitedly with Michelle toward a goal important to both of us.

• • •

2

One Final Lesson

On February 1, 2007, Michael was a fourteen-year-old enjoying his last year at Hillside Middle School. Benjamin was eleven and attended Highland Park Elementary School along with Anna, who was then nine. Sam, six, was in half-day kindergarten. It had been fifteen years since we had purchased our starter home. We loved where we lived; our family roots were quite established in the neighborhood, which made it hard to consider moving anywhere else. We also appreciated that the size of our home imposed a sense of financial discipline on us. Even if we wanted to buy more stuff, there was physically no room. We never thought our home was too small for more children, and Michelle was now expecting our fifth child. We knew that some of our neighbors had moved into our area in the 1940s, when these homes were considered larger homes—ones occupied after people moved from starter homes. We figured if they could raise large families here, we should certainly be able to as well.

This fifth child we were expecting was a tremendous blessing.

After Sam's birth, Michelle and I had wanted at least one more child, but she was concerned that because of the miscarriage complications she had experienced in the past she would not be able to have any more children. As I prayed, asking for her to receive a blessing of comfort to her soul, we received a confirmation from the Holy Spirit that she would have another baby. Our faith in that blessing was tested as she endured two more miscarriages. One of those came after I had been called as a bishop, which is a lay minister in our religious congregation of over four hundred members. We initially thought that the pregnancy was a blessing for our willingness to serve; however, after the miscarriage, we knew that it was a different type of blessing. It became yet another opportunity for us to have our faith in Jesus Christ strengthened.

In her faithful persistence to not give up, Michelle was continually researching what she could do differently to reduce the risk of miscarriage. She found a study that indicated taking a baby aspirin while pregnant could reduce clotting in the umbilical cord and prevent the type of miscarriages she was experiencing. After consulting with her physician when she again became pregnant, she started that simple regimen and everything progressed perfectly. We found it so fascinating that the answer to all of those terrible trials was so simple and inexpensive, a small baby aspirin. In February she was less than four months away from delivery.

At one ultrasound appointment to check on the health of the baby, we left with pictures of the baby in the womb, including one picture of a perfect little hand almost in the shape of a "thumbs up" sign. This baby was going to be okay! It had been nearly six years from the time I had been prompted to promise Michelle she would have another baby, and now we were anxious to welcome our fifth child into our family, a baby boy we were planning to name William Dorny Williams.

• • •

We were incredibly blessed to have been surrounded with wonderful friends and neighbors. One of our children's favorite neighbors was the Arrowsmith family, who lived across from our house. Duane, or "Dewey" as he preferred to be called, and his wife, Charlene, were an older couple who had lived in the neighborhood for nearly forty years. If we couldn't find our children in our house, the first place we would look for them was across the street at Dewey and Charlene's house. Typically we would find them deep in conversation with Dewey about school, the weather, or what sport the children were currently pursuing, all the while enjoying some candy and playing with his dog, Kimi. Sam especially loved to visit Dewey and Kimi. For a six-year-old as gregarious as Sam, perhaps there wasn't anything better than a place where you could engage in lively chat with an entertaining neighbor, have some candy, and then enjoy playing with a very pleasant dog when there was a pause in the conversation. We were thankful to have such a wonderful neighbor and friend, especially for our children.

Dewey passed away on February 3, 2007. When we broke the news to Sam that Dewey had died, he didn't initially understand what we were talking about; no one close to him had ever died before. Michelle, Sam, and I went to the viewing, which is a visitation with the family prior to the funeral. After we paid our respects to Charlene and other family members, Sam sat down in a chair close to where Dewey lay. Rather than move Sam from where the family had also gathered, Michelle sat by him and let him continue his close, careful observation of Dewey. After some time, he turned to Michelle and asked, "When is he going to wake up?"

I started to think of something funny to say, but Michelle was much wiser and saw the opportunity to teach. She looked at Sam and began to talk about the gospel, or "good news," regarding death, that everyone will be resurrected and live again.

Michelle explained our belief that when we die, our spirit goes back to the spirit world and our body stays here, and that one day both will be reunited again because Jesus Christ made that possible. I watched as she took one of my gloves and demonstrated to Sam that a glove is like our body and that our hand is like the spirit, and that when we're born, it's like putting a hand into a glove so that the body can move by obeying the command of the spirit. She explained that when we die, it's like taking the hand out of the glove, and the body stays here, unable to move without the spirit.

Sam looked back at Dewey in the casket and simply said, "Ah, that makes sense." He didn't have any other questions, and he didn't indicate the slightest bit of concern about what was going on after that. His mother had given him all he needed for his believing six-year-old heart to know about one of the most profound doctrines, that all will be resurrected after they die. It was a tremendous opportunity for Michelle to teach one of her children the important truth about what happens when someone dies.

• • •

3

Four Giving Hearts

February 9, 2007, was on a Friday. There had never been anything memorable or terribly remarkable about that day for any of us. That particular Friday in February was in many ways so similar to the Friday before it, or just about any other Friday afternoon in the Williams's household with our four children.

Fridays typically meant a "short day"—teachers were given preparation time to get their lessons ready for the next week—so during the school year, children came home earlier than usual on those days. Our home was always filled with vibrant activity and constant motion and noise upon the return of our kids from school, perhaps in eager anticipation for the weekend or because they were simply relieved the school week had come to an end. Since friends frequently accompanied them home, the sound of laughter, music, doors and kitchen cabinets opening and closing, and footsteps on the wood floors and elsewhere as the kids ran around made our home one of the noisiest, yet most "at peace" places on earth.

My job as a sales manager for a technology company allowed me to work from home, and I was privileged to experience the commotion each Friday afternoon from my basement office, unless I was on a conference call. Then I deftly worked the mute button before I emerged from my cave of an office and tried to persuade my children to be quiet. However, I typically blocked out some time each Friday afternoon to interact with the children as they came home, partly to be with them and partly because trying to shush children who had been in school all week and who were ready to have some fun never really worked that well. On this particular Friday, Anna and Sam burst into my office as soon as they came home from school, eager to show me the valentines they had created at school for Michelle and me.

Early in the evening I drove Sam to a friend's home to play for a little while and then took Michael to Highland High School, where he was meeting friends to attend a school basketball game. Upon returning home, I went downstairs where Michelle was relaxing with Anna. Our daughter had a very active imagination. When she was barely able to walk, she would get a rock from the garden, swaddle it the best she could in a small blanket, and walk around tenderly with her pet rock baby. She was a gifted peacemaker, always encouraging her three brothers to love each other, have patience, and remember that, regardless of the problem, "it will be okay."

I entered our family room and saw Michelle and Anna watching *Animal Planet* on TV. It was Anna's favorite show. She loved animals and had already decided she wanted to be a veterinarian when she grew up. For Anna it wasn't just idle TV time; this was career preparation, and after each show she loved to talk about the animals she learned about. Ben was seated on the couch close to Michelle, though not terribly focused on the TV show. He always seemed to have multiple things going on at once. He loved to be in the spotlight—the center of attention—yet he seemed to be waiting in the wings that night, getting ready to take the stage.

Knowing Michelle had been fairly tired because of the pregnancy, I suggested we go to dinner at a local Mexican restaurant, a family favorite close to home. Anna asked if she could finish *Animal Planet* first. Earlier in the week she had decorated the inside of her valentine's box with a bunch of dogs; I thought maybe she was watching to see what additional animals she should add. I went back into my office to wait for the show to end at 8:00 P.M. We were in no particular hurry that Friday night.

After *Animal Planet* ended, Michelle, Anna, Ben, and I drove to the restaurant. We had just ordered when our neighbors Mike and Jennifer Purdy and their son Liam entered the restaurant. We motioned for them to join us, and Ben quickly jumped up to move another table next to ours so that he could sit by one of his close friends. It was as if the curtains had opened; Ben was onstage performing for the whole table. This was Ben's typical behavior, finding joy and humor in just about everything he did, and here he was giving one of his best performances—telling funny stories, laughing at his own stories, and then asking me if I thought he was funny. I was laughing quite hard, so the answer that night was naturally a resounding yes.

Usually I would counsel him not to be too silly in public, or give him a look a mature parent might send as a note of caution, even though the eleven-year-old in me thought he was very funny and wanted him to keep going. That night I just loved him. He was especially adorable and comical; I laughed at all of his stories, and I didn't try to dampen his love of life.

Ben was recalling his antics earlier in the day. He had

participated in the school ski program, which meant he had been snowboarding for a half day at a local ski resort. After the kids returned to the school, Michelle parked at the pick-up zone and was waiting for Ben while he loaded his equipment and said an extended good-bye to his friends. Finally, Michelle rolled down the passenger window and hollered for Ben to get in. He quickly turned from his friends, ran toward the car, and dove into the front passenger seat through the open window. He made it halfway in and milked the comedic effect by letting his feet dangle out while the car started to pull forward, and then he slowly pulled himself the rest of the way into the front seat. I'm sure his friends and the other mothers waiting must have enjoyed the performance as so many were familiar with his exuberant personality.

His silliness notwithstanding, Michelle and I had always known we were blessed with a spiritual giant. The previous fall Ben's Little League football team had played for the conference championship and lost. As the team huddled away from the parents for a final meeting after the game, I could see from a distance that many of the players were quite upset and angry because of the loss. Ben left the meeting and walked toward me, attempting to hide his tears. I put my arm around him and began to encourage him by saying, "Well, you did your best, and there's always next year."

He looked at me and said, "I'm not crying because we lost. One of the kids took the Lord's name in vain, and I told him that wasn't cool."

Ben was a remarkable child.

• • •

Anna sat politely and quietly during the meal; she wasn't a big fan of the traditional Mexican fare, but she was such a good sport to come along. She too had an enormous gift for loving life, and she had such a fun and creative imagination, but on this particular night she simply sat back and reveled in Ben's stories and laughter. Usually when we ate dinner with friends, the adults would gather at one end of the table and the children at the other. That evening, however, Michelle was talking with the Purdys, and I sat across from Anna and right by Ben. I can still see Anna and her incredibly blue eyes and hear Ben's laughter and see how very happy he was. I admired both of them so much, and I was as content as any father could be to be blessed with such incredible children. I didn't sense anything; I had no foreboding whatsoever. I was inclined to just watch them and love them for who they were, unconditionally.

After dinner we picked up Sam, who was finished playing at his friend's house, and then decided as a family to get some dessert before returning home. One of our favorite quick treats was a vanilla ice cream cone at a local fast-food place just minutes from our house. To get there we needed to travel a road called the I 80 underpass, an unremarkable small stretch of road that dips below the I-80 freeway. It is a road I had travelled hundreds of times in my life; there was nothing to indicate this time would be any different. I don't recall feeling any prompting to adjust our travel in some way, to spend a few more seconds at a stop sign, to take an alternate route, or to just go straight home. In an instant, our lives were about to change forever.

• • •

4

A Terrible Tragedy

I drove to the top of Stratford Avenue and 2000 East, turned north, and proceeded to drive under the I-80 freeway. Before you descend under this particular underpass, the freeway is at eye level and obscures the lights of the oncoming traffic. About halfway down the hill, you can then see the lights from the cars headed in your direction. Our car was moving at about thirty miles an hour, well within the speed limit. Michelle and I both saw a pair of headlights appear at the top of the hill in front of us, moving at an unbelievably high rate of speed. The vehicle was already crossing the median and was on a direct collision course with our car. I heard Michelle shout, "Chris!" and I attempted to swerve out of the way to avoid being hit but to no avail.

In the court proceedings after the crash, it was shown that we didn't have a chance. The oncoming car never attempted to slow down. At the last second, the driver overcorrected to avoid crashing into the bridge support pillars, and his car T-boned our car, striking it directly in the rear passenger door. The force was so violent and tremendous that the impact stopped our car from going downhill and pushed it back uphill and toward the bridge supports on the opposite side of the roadway. The sound of the car hitting ours was a sickening, dense, crushing thud of metal on metal—a quick, catastrophic, singular sound of devastation.

Immediately after the impact, my mind was active and aware that we had been hit, but I couldn't hear anything nor could I see anything but a blinding, brilliant white that appeared to encompass me. The light didn't seem to have any single point from which it came; everything that I was conscious and aware of was immersed in a luminous whiteness. The sensation of being surrounded by silence and white dissipated like a fog slowly lifting. I could perceive what looked like very fine snow falling in front of me and around the car; later I decided it was perhaps the finer pieces of the exploded windshield now falling gently back to earth. I began to hear a noise that sounded faint at first but which grew progressively louder. It was a high-pitched, strained, mechanical sound coming from a car engine being revved at its highest rate; I sensed that my right leg was fully depressing the accelerator pedal.

Fearing that we would explode with the engine revving so high, I tried to move my leg off the pedal, but it wouldn't respond to my attempts to move it. I tried to move my hand forward to turn the car off, and I immediately felt excruciating pain. I knew then that I was significantly injured. I struggled to work my hand progressively forward, and I finally turned the ignition key off. The airbag had deployed, and the dash had been pushed toward me. My mind was racing to process what had just happened; we had been critically hit by whatever had been speeding toward us.

There was no sound from anyone in the car. I could see Michelle was motionless and curled up in a fetal position on the

Site of car crash, February 9, 2007 (the Williams's car is on the right)

passenger seat; her hair was draped over her face so that I couldn't see it at all. I desperately struggled to move my hand onto hers, to feel for a pulse. I couldn't sense a heartbeat through her hand. As I continued to search her wrist for a pulse, I saw her other arm closest to her door. She had a significant wound on her elbow that wasn't bleeding; it looked like it had been blown open from the inside, and I could see bone and tissue, but no blood. In that instant, I knew that she was gone. In my state of shock, still struggling to comprehend what had just happened, that thought was so clear and definitive. It didn't come from deductive reasoning, it was just pure knowledge of a terrible reality, that no amount of CPR or emergency assistance would help her—she was gone. My thoughts raced to my children in the backseat, *were they okay?*

I physically struggled to turn my head, frantically trying to move so I could check on the condition of my children. Ben was sitting directly behind Michelle and was the first child I was able

to see. He was sitting upright, his head resting against the im-
ploded car door. He had a significant gash on his head, exposing
his skull, and I could see that the wound wasn't bleeding. Once
again, I experienced the same type of immediate understanding
regarding his condition, that he was gone. I just felt it. I struggled
to turn further to see Anna who was sitting in the middle back
seat. She was sitting upright but leaning slightly forward, with her
hair draped over her head so I couldn't see her face. I couldn't see
any physical injury whatsoever; she looked like she had just fallen
asleep. But before I could even begin to think that she might be
okay and might have survived the impact, I once again instantly
knew that she too was gone. With that final revelation as to their
deaths, I also knew that that was the extent—I couldn't see Sam
nor could I hear him, but I didn't think to be worried or concerned or to call out for him or try to see if he was alive or dead.

As I stopped straining to see into the backseat, I turned my
head toward Michelle and I saw her chest sink down. She hadn't
been breathing, but that was it, one final exhale, and then I
thought of our baby.

What I was witnessing was so absolutely unreal. I couldn't
take it anymore; I turned my head forward and closed my eyes;
I was ready for death. I tried to will myself to pass out; I wanted
to succumb to the process of having my spirit leave my body. The
more I tried to let go and die, the more I became aware of a terrible, "other worldly" sound that was growing louder and louder,
interrupting my thoughts and my desire to pass to the other
side. The sound wasn't coming from the car or the surroundings,
although I was aware that by then there were people outside the
car. I even remember hearing someone exclaim, "Oh no, there are
children inside!" No, this sound was coming from right where
I sat, not from my throat, but from deep inside my body. I was

the one making that horrific sound—that sound of excruciating anguish and pain, of a body and a spirit being crushed.

It was more profound than just feeling helpless or powerless or feeling physical pain. It was a brief, nearly out-of-body moment in which I felt completely undone. My soul was under such intense pressure, my heart was broken, and my spirit was beyond contrite; I was absolutely crushed. I struggled to make the sound stop; there was such pain and agony in the noise that I couldn't take it. I opened my eyes and turned to look out the driver's side window. I saw the car that had just hit us resting upside down on its roof about fifty feet uphill from my car. The horrific sound ceased as did the voices outside the car; there was suddenly an immense peace and silence that filled the inside of the vehicle, my soul, and my thoughts.

I had no idea who had just hit us, and my mind didn't think to consider if they were all right or not, or what circumstances might have caused them to cross the median and strike us. I simply looked at the car in silence. My thoughts went quiet, I felt at peace, and then I heard a voice that was not my own in my mind as clearly as if it had come from someone seated next to me. It wasn't a peaceful, whispered voice, nor was it the still, small prompting of the Spirit; it was straightforward and filled with power, and the voice said, "Let it go!"

I didn't turn my head toward where I perceived the voice to be coming from; I fixed my eyes on the overturned car. I immediately felt an enabling power beyond my own, healing and enlarging my crushed and receptive soul. I knew exactly what I had to do and exactly what those three words meant. Regardless of whoever had been driving the other car and regardless of whatever the circumstances behind this tragedy were, this was not my burden to carry. I was told in no uncertain terms not to try to pick it up.

I understood that this was not an invitation to let it go, this was a direct command to let it go.

My soul had just been exposed to such pain that I knew in the brief feeling of utter nothingness I had been allowed to experience that I had no power to even try to take this burden at all. I committed as I sat in that driver's seat—looking at the car that had just killed my wife, Michelle; our baby, William; my son Benjamin; and my daughter, Anna—to let it go, all of it, holding nothing back. This was not my burden to carry, and I would be crushed no more. I knew who would carry that burden: He who had already endured the soul crushing press of the pains of all men, including this burden, so that I would not have to bear my infinitely miniscule portion of what He bore. In that instant of grace and revelation, I knew that my Savior lived, that He was immediately present with me in my time of greatest need, with healing in His wings.

The peace and strength that accompanied the commitment I made further reinforced the decision. I turned to look back at Michelle and noticed how peaceful she looked. There was no blood, no gore, only my beautiful, gracious wife curled up on the passenger seat as if she were asleep, her hair gently veiling her face, completely covering it.

I turned toward my wonderful son Benjamin who was seated upright. He looked so peaceful and calm as he leaned against the car door. Then I looked at Anna, her head forward with her hair draped completely over her face; my sweet Anna—so gentle, patient, kind, and always encouraging. As I looked upon her, I didn't need to see her face to feel who she was. It was as if angels had prepared that scene for my private final viewing of my family while they passed to the other side. Those images and the recollection of that last good-bye are still so vivid in my mind;

they remain one of the sweetest tender mercies that I have ever received.

As I continued to privately view my family, it seemed as if I had been in that car a near eternity. The *Deseret News* interviewed Michael Lee, who was one of the people outside my car that night. In that report, Lee expressed frustration with how long it took the police and paramedics to arrive at the crash site. Minutes felt like hours before a fire engine finally arrived, the *News* reported. "It was an excruciating wait," Lee said. I'm satisfied that emergency crews arrived as quickly as they could. I needed that time, however, to learn and experience truths that I could learn in no other way to prepare me for the difficult journey ahead. I also needed that time to say good-bye, for now.

I continued to observe the state of my family in that surreal, yet peaceful scene when suddenly the driver-side door popped open, and a hand hurriedly reached around me to undo my seat belt, while others were positioning my head for a neck brace. Now there was a great deal of commotion all around me as I was prepared to be taken from the car. At that moment, amidst the commotion, I heard Samuel cry out from the back of the car. Not once after realizing that Anna, Ben, and Michelle had passed away, and receiving the peace regarding Sam, had I thought to be concerned about him again or wonder if he would make it, even though the cry Sam made was as horrific and pained as the one I had previously made after the crash. As I was placed into a waiting ambulance, I knew that I didn't need to worry about my little Sammy and that he would not be alone. His mother would be with him, and she would take perfect care of him.

• • •

5

To Be Willing Is to Be Tested

During the ambulance ride to the hospital, emergency crews asked me question after question to keep me alert and responding to them. They began to cut away clothes, start IVs, and assess my vital signs. My neck was in a brace, and it was hard to look around. As calm as I tried to remain in the back of the ambulance, the ride was terrifying as I became more and more aware of the pain that I was in. Not being able to move as I lay on the hard backboard and not being able to look around because of the neck brace didn't help matters either. I coughed and immediately felt a sharp, piercing pain on my right side. As I inhaled after the cough, I had the feeling that my lungs were starting to fill with water, as if I were slowly drowning. I started to pray for relief, but the pain grew in intensity with each subsequent cough, and the water seemed to be rising faster in my lungs. I prayed harder as I once again felt so very helpless and increasingly all alone.

I was wheeled into the emergency room of the University of Utah Medical Center, with the faces of medical and emergency personnel coming into and out of my field of view. The gurney came to a stop, and within minutes I saw some familiar faces. My cousin Brian Monson and his wife, Heidi, were there. They had been told of the crash by someone who was on the scene right after the impact and who knew we were related. Brian and Heidi had immediately raced to the hospital to be with me—certainly in response to my prayer said in the ambulance, as the peace I had experienced in the car returned when I saw them. Brian took my cell phone from my pants pocket and started calling through my list of phone numbers to let people know what had happened.

As others received the news, they too raced to the hospital to be with me. Soon the faces of other friends and loved ones started to come into my field of view as I lay on my back, unable to move. Seeing each person brought additional strength as I continued to receive medical attention and tried to manage the terrible pain I was experiencing.

When there was a break in the medical commotion around me, James Wood, my stake president (another ecclesiastical lay position) and friend, stepped forward and informed me that our car had been hit by a teenage boy who had apparently been drinking. My initial reaction upon hearing how this terrible tragedy had come to pass was to ask him if the boy was all right. James said that the boy was okay and that he didn't appear to have sustained any physical injury.

I then asked James if he would please have the young man's name placed on the temple prayer roll. (This is a list of names of individuals needing blessings and peace that are regularly prayed for by disciples of Jesus Christ.)

The request about the temple prayer roll was an echo from an experience I had had as a teenager. When I was sixteen years old, driving to work at the LDS Hospital, two young boys ran between parked cars and into the path of my car. I never even saw them come into the street; I heard only the noise of something striking my car. I was driving under the speed limit, I certainly hadn't been drinking, I wasn't distracted in any way, and no charges were filed. It was in every respect just an accident, yet as I sat all alone in the police car during the investigation, a woman opened the police car door and asked me if I would like my name placed on the temple prayer roll.

As a sixteen-year-old, I was familiar with the Salt Lake Temple, but I didn't know how a temple prayer roll was used or what that even meant. Her suggestion of the temple—and by extension, comfort from Jesus Christ—brought such healing to me then, that in my circumstance following the crash, realizing that it was a teenage boy that had hit our car, my thoughts were taken right back to that moment in my life, this time with a desire to be like that woman who had brought such hope into my life. It seems as though the concept of "paying it forward" certainly does have a heavenly origin at times.

• • •

As I lay on that gurney, I could feel the love the Savior had for that teenage boy. It was a soul-transforming and refining experience. I had a sure confidence that the collective faith of thousands of those worshiping regularly in the temple, praying for that teenage boy, would bring the needed correction, guidance, and blessings into the life of that young man.

Struggling for breath with fluid in my lungs and thinking of the deaths of my wife, our unborn child, and two of my four children, I was blessed with a power beyond my own to see that moment for what it really was: my first test to see if I would stay true to the commitment I had just made while seated in the car after the crash. My request of James Wood was a very public way of demonstrating to my Father in Heaven, Michelle, Ben, and Anna that I was not going to break that commitment.

I was in pain, yet I felt peace; I was carrying an enormous new weight, yet I was unburdened; I was in the midst of a swarm of activity and unable to move, yet I had an eternal perspective that was peaceful and liberating.

Another friend, Michael Hennessey, came near to where I lay. I looked at him as earnestly as I could and said, "We have to forgive him." I felt no anger, no desire for retribution or justice, no questioning as to why this had happened, just an earnest desire to say the things the Savior would say, extending the same tokens of mercy and love that He always extends.

I had no idea who the teenager was. I didn't know his name although I would later find out his initials were the same as mine, that he went to the same high school I had, that he played on the same football team, and that he drove a white SUV similar to one I had in high school. I didn't know that he and his family lived a few houses away from Michelle's parents, that his siblings lived in my neighborhood, or that his uncle would be one of the physicians working on Sam in the hospital. All I felt in that moment was that the Savior had succored or run to me, anxious to heal and bind up rather than have this crash tear up our families and the community.

The emergency room doctors continued to assess my condition, specifically concerned about the possibility of internal bleeding. There seemed to be so many doctors and nurses coming into and going out of my line of sight, each performing a specific assignment or role. As the assessment progressed, my observation of their work was interrupted by a very painful poke into my side. I looked right at the physician who was doing those evaluations and exclaimed aloud, "Hello!" My reaction and comment brought a slight smile to my face and caught me a bit off guard. That I would even think to say something that brought some levity into the moment was just miraculous. In hindsight, I guess I needed something to prepare me for the next face that came into my view.

When I saw my son Michael entering the emergency room, I broke down and started crying, even though I wanted to be strong for him. He too was crying hard. I'll never forget that look on his face of such pain, grief, and shock. It was overwhelming to me as his father to see him suffering, and I felt so very helpless, unable to hold him and comfort him or help him in any way. He was taken to a waiting room near the ER, and there he was prayed for and comforted by friends and family. Michael has since recounted how he felt a majestic peace accompany him as he sat in that waiting room, and he was assured of the love the Savior had for him and that he need not despair. Yet, even with the strength we felt, this was truly anyone's worst nightmare come to life.

• • •

6

A Refined Torture

The doctors couldn't conclusively rule out internal bleeding
in the emergency room, but they felt that I was stable enough to
be moved to the Intensive Care Unit (ICU). I was given a morphine pump to self-manage the pain in my ribs. I was instructed
that the pump would deliver the medicine through my IV when
I pushed the pump button. Initially I thought I didn't want any
morphine, but it took only one or two coughs accompanied
by that piercing pain for me to start pushing the button pretty
quickly to administer the relief. After several button presses,
however, I began to wonder if I hadn't been given some sort of
dummy device to placate me or distract me, as it didn't seem to
be making any difference in the pain.

I hurt terribly all over my body; I prayed before each cough
that I wouldn't cough, that I could be delivered somehow from
this terrible situation, perhaps even miraculously, and I tried to
muster as much faith as possible for something like that to happen. More visitors, all in shock, came into the ICU to see me.

They didn't know what to say to me, and conversing with them was too physically painful. As the stream of people increased, the image of an atomic-bomb shockwave came into my mind, as if the crash impact had sent a shockwave through the community and everyone was feeling and reacting to the effects. I prayed for Michael and Sam, but I never felt concerned for Sam's physical condition or the possibility that I might lose him too; I just felt a continued assurance that he was going to make it, that he would be healed completely.

I tried to be a source of strength to the visitors who came into my room and assure them that all would be well, that in the midst of this terrible tragedy there would be hope. I continued to struggle through the acute pain and the liquid in my lungs, but mentally I started to shut down. I felt that I had endured too much and I couldn't be strong anymore. I wanted to be left alone, so I started to feign sleep just so people would stop coming into my room to see me. I didn't want to show any weakness, but I couldn't be there for them anymore. When I appeared to be falling asleep, the nurses ushered those around me out of the room and prevented others who had yet to come in from entering. The lights in the room were turned off, the door was closed, and I was left alone and wide-awake.

I wanted Michelle so desperately. I couldn't see her, I couldn't feel her or talk to her, and I didn't know what to do. I had felt peace and I could pray, but I needed her because she was a part of me, and I had never felt that separation before. The pain of the broken bones and the discomfort of the fluid in my lungs were nothing compared to the pain of separation I felt that night. And there I lay in that bed, wide-awake and so terribly alone.

My pain and grief were interrupted when I heard an IV alarm sound in the next room. The alarm made the same horrible, grating beeping noise that my alarm clock at home made. After beeping for a seeming eternity, the IV alarm was suddenly quiet. All night long that IV alarm would go off without warning, and then it would eventually be silenced. I couldn't believe that it was the *exact* same sound. Looking for any levity in such a terrible moment I thought, *Where do they manufacture those irritating alarms?* I figured it had to be in bulk if they found their way into clocks and IV systems. I wondered if the person who was in charge of testing those alarms wasn't horribly depressed. But as I lay in that bed, unable to silence the alarm when it did go off, I was forced to endure it for as long as it took some unseen individual to silence it. Sometimes that was rather quickly, and sometimes it didn't seem quick at all. There were no additional minutes of sleep, no victory over the alarm to start the day; I didn't feel I could go to sleep regardless of how much I wanted to. Michelle wasn't lying by my side anymore, quietly and patiently enduring the noise. It was an exquisite and refined affliction, genius in its tormenting perfection, given the circumstances I was enduring. I will admit that it would have been a very just payback had I later found out that Michelle was somehow in the next room setting off the alarm and then silencing it.

Each time I tried to force myself to drift into sleep, the alarm in the next room would sound. At some point I must have been falling asleep because when I would be awakened by the alarm, in my startled yet drowsy state, I would look around to see if the entire evening had indeed been a terrible dream. *Maybe I am really just back in my bed at home experiencing the worst nightmare of my life*, I thought. Then I would cough, feel the stabbing pain and the fluid in my lungs, and know that this was indeed a real nightmare that I was experiencing, and there was no escaping it by sleeping or waking.

Early the next morning when the nurses came in to check on me, I asked them to let my family come back into the room. I was taken to be X-rayed to ensure I didn't have any internal bleeding or unseen injuries that might need attention. The X-rays showed that I had sustained a broken rib on my right side and nothing else, no indications of internal bleeding or organ damage. I remember thinking, *The injuries my family sustained were so catastrophic, and all I have is a broken rib?* Autopsies would later show that Michelle, Ben, and Anna's hearts became detached from their main arteries due to the impact; their hearts were literally broken. And all I had was a broken rib? I felt guilty for feeling that I had been more damaged than I was. As I marveled at the lack of internal damage, I had an impression that I had been preserved, quite miraculously, so I could be with Michael and Sam while Michelle was with Ben and Anna. Perhaps that sense of "whiteness" I felt after the crash was as close as I got to the other side. The feelings of guilt departed, and I was left with no reason for me to stay there with just a broken rib; I immediately wanted out of the ICU. The attending doctors met with me and advised me to stay one more night for observation, but I refused. I had to be with Michael and Sam. I could no longer bear being separated from them, and I would not endure another night in that bed with that terrible alarm going off over and over and being so very alone.

My parents, Paul and Nadine, and my brothers, David and Fred, and my sister, Sara, had stayed at the hospital through the night, and it was a huge comfort to see them and have their love and support. They had brought some clothes from my house for me to wear. When I took off the hospital gown to get dressed, I was shocked to see that my torso was black and blue nearly everywhere. I had shards of glass stuck into the skin on my back, which I had been lying on since I had been taken out of the car. With my father's assistance, we cleaned the blood and the glass off my skin, and I got dressed. We left the ICU and walked from the University Medical Center through a connecting hallway to Primary Children's Medical Center, where Sam had been taken.

We entered the children's ICU, and I was taken to the bed where Sam lay. I was shocked to see his condition. Even though I had felt peace that he was going to be all right, I was told he was in critical condition. He had suffered a serious brain injury, and his condition was not improving. The doctors had drilled a small hole in his forehead through which a bolt device was inserted to measure cranial pressure. I became faint. His neck was in a brace, he had a cut on his right ear, his lips were swollen, and he had a broken rib and a broken collar bone. But the biggest concern was that he had experienced bleeding deep in his brain and, if the cranial pressure didn't go down, he might suffer permanent brain damage. He made the most horrid cry when he had to cough or when he felt pain. It was haunting to see my little Sammy in such pain, and I felt so devastated and again so alone without Michelle as I hovered over him in the hospital bed. I could relate with part of the pain he was feeling as it appeared he had the same stabbing pain after each cough that I had, along with some fluid in his lungs.

I quickly arranged to give him a blessing of health, accompanied by my dad and Michelle's father, Gordon Dorny. As we prayed, a surge of peace and confidence filled my soul. I felt assured he would make a full recovery. It wasn't wishful thinking on my part; I felt I knew exactly what the Savior wanted me to say and what he would have said had he been there in person. At the conclusion of the blessing, I also knew that Sammy wouldn't spring right out of the bed. Although his physical healing would indeed be quick, it would also be measured to provide the best possible outcome for him.

The opportunity to know and pronounce what the Savior would say if he were there came because of my willingness to have faith in whatever the will of the Lord was, even if it was that Sam would pass away. I guess I was prepared for this opportunity to bless Sam because of an experience I had had several years earlier with Michael. After a family trip to Chicago in the fall of 2005, Michael somehow contracted septicemia, or blood poisoning. I was at work when I received the phone call that his organs were shutting down, that "it didn't look good," and that he was in an ambulance on his way to Primary Children's Medical Center.

As I drove there to be with him, I knew that one of the first things I would do upon arriving would be to give him a blessing of health. As I prayed en route to the hospital to know the will of the Lord, I recall asking that if Michael was to be healed, that I would be able to pronounce that with confidence. But I also felt prompted to ask that if we were going to lose Michael, that Michelle and I might be given the strength to endure his death. In that prayer about Michael, inspired by the Spirit, I was reminded of an important lesson in seeking the will of the Lord, that I had to be completely open to whatever that will or counsel was going to be. Was I truly willing to submit to all things? As soon as I finished my prayer, I received an assurance in my mind that Michael would indeed be healed completely, and I knew during the blessing exactly what the outcome would be.

● ● ●

After giving Sam a blessing, Michael and I stayed by his bed-side that entire evening in the children's ICU. I held his little hand, looked at his face, and cried. He would cough or move and then cry out in pain, and his cranial pressure would spike, which wasn't desirable. Then the nurses would get worried and talk about adjusting the treatment to keep the pressure down so his brain wasn't permanently damaged. As I began to ponder further on the blessing given, that I had been assured that Sam would be healed, I began to think it was more akin to Moses holding up his arms until the Red Sea had parted, watching until he was obeyed. I sensed that I would have to watch that blessing come to pass with faith, nothing doubting, until Sammy was completely healed, especially since it appeared that his situation was getting worse. I had to exercise my faith.

I again prayed so hard for Michelle to be there with me too; I felt that Sam and Michael needed both their parents to be with them. I desperately wanted some sense of her presence. *Why wouldn't she be allowed to be with her son,* I thought. As my frustration grew because I hadn't yet felt any confirmation that she was there to support me, I had an impression that Michelle, Ben, and Anna did know of our circumstances, and they knew we would be well cared for, but that they wanted me to go through this relying wholly on the Savior's grace, which is his enabling power. There was no other way I would be able to make it through. I was reminded that the Holy Spirit is the appointed Comforter, not the spirit of a deceased spouse, and that I should stop bugging Michelle and the children; they were busy upon their arrival in heaven.

· · ·

7

"Buck Up, Charlie"

Later that evening, my neighbor Mike Purdy came into the children's ICU to be with me and to check on Sam. Mike told me that I wouldn't believe "what's going on out there." He talked about the incredibly moving effect that this tragedy was having on the community and what the news media was saying about the crash and my offer of forgiveness toward the teenage driver. Since my thoughts were wholly focused on what was going on with Sammy, I didn't fully grasp what he was talking about. It wasn't until the next day, Sunday, that I found out that what I had said as I lay on the gurney about forgiving the teenage driver had been reported in the media, and it was impacting the entire community, even in the face of the terrible circumstances.

Although the press attributed this outcome to what I had said, I knew that the forgiveness and mercy was extended by the Savior, and that I had simply benefited from His strength when He spoke through me. I had experienced my weaknesses when I was left to my own abilities, so I was fully aware of who was in charge of the many miracles that were starting to transpire, of the souls that were being touched, and of the lives that were being changed. I was struck by the thought that Michelle, Ben, and Anna were probably right then busy influencing other lives that needed to be touched and healed because of the crash, and that they were on their first angelic errands to minister. I could see how my pleadings for them to be with Michael, Sam, and me were perhaps distracting. *Dad, we love you, but we're very busy* was the thought that came to my mind from my wonderful family, even though it wasn't initially what I wanted to hear.

• • •

That Saturday night, the nurses pulled curtains around Sam's bed to give us more privacy as we prepared to get some sleep. Before I could try to get some rest, I knew I had to speak with my Father in Heaven in prayer. Since the crash I had petitioned Him frequently in silent prayers of my heart, yet I now yearned to converse with Him out loud and at length.

I left Sam and Michael, who were being attended to by other members of the family, and began looking for an appropriate place to hold that conversation. I walked into the visitors' lounge and entered one of the small side rooms. It was the size of a large closet, and a solitary chair and a small bed completely filled the room. I entered the room, closed the door, and turned off the light. I knelt down on the floor and began to weep as I started to pray aloud. The anguish of soul that I had felt in the car returned, yet it was now multiplied by a sense of being so alone. The harder I wept, the more compression I felt in my soul—it was terrible and dark.

But as I pleaded for help, a wonderful peace filled the room.

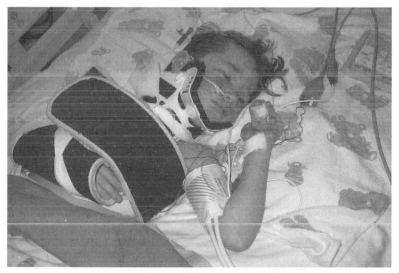

Sam in Primary Children's Medical Center

My heart softened, I stopped crying, and my thoughts quieted. I heard a very familiar voice in my mind, and I opened my eyes to see if she were there speaking to me. It was Michelle's voice saying, "Buck up, Charlie!"—an instruction that she had frequently given me during our marriage whenever I had complained or whined about something to her, or when I had felt things were just too tough. I'll admit there were times when her chiding only made things worse, but those times usually ended with me conceding that the only thing worse than being stupid was to be stupid and wrong. This time, as soon as I heard that phrase in my mind, I smiled, knowing that she was right once again. She had just successfully called me on the carpet in a way only a loving spouse could.

I knew I had to keep moving forward. I reached up and turned on the light. My thoughts immediately shifted from how terrible I felt to how grateful I was. I continued my prayer, but now I was expressing my love for my Father in Heaven in helping me to marry someone as incredible as Michelle and for blessing me with such a deep and abiding love for her.

My mind quickly started to recall experience after experience with her, some touching, some funny, others so very tender and personal. I was so thankful for everything I had been given because of her. I thought of my children—first Ben, then Anna—remembering so many sweet experiences and expressing my gratitude for each one. I was thankful that they were safe and with her. My next thoughts were of Michael and Sam. I felt such gratitude for the assurance I had been given that they would be taken care of and that they would be blessed throughout their lives because of what they were being asked to pass through. And then my thoughts turned to the Savior.

I was nearly overcome as I tried to thank my Father in Heaven for allowing His Son to die for me, that my Savior and Redeemer had suffered the will of the Father in all things. I thought, too, of my Father in Heaven and His willingness to not intervene to stop the suffering of His Son. As I wept, my words and thoughts failed to convey the desire I had to express a sufficient gratitude for the atonement of Jesus Christ. I pleaded for forgiveness because of my shortcomings in my inability to adequately communicate that gratitude. As my prayer drew to a close, I considered what I might ask my Father in Heaven for as I knelt in his presence. At that moment, I had a stupor of thought; I couldn't think of anything to request. I had been given every eternal assurance I needed. I concluded the prayer, peeled back the covers on the small bed, and crawled inside.

• • •

8

Lean on Me

I slept for perhaps an hour that night. But when I pushed off the covers and moved to get out of the bed, I felt a popping sensation in my rib cage, as if the broken rib had burst through the surrounding muscle, and an excruciating pain shot through my side. I realized I couldn't move and no one knew where I was. I couldn't breathe deeply enough to yell out, so I relaxed as much as possible while I tried to think of what to do. One of my crazy thoughts was that I wished I had one of those alert devices around my neck to tell someone that I couldn't get up. I had mocked those TV commercials many times, but now I really could have used one of those alerts. Eventually I used my hands and feet to slowly shimmy toward the foot of the bed where I slid off the mattress and plopped onto the floor. I arose slowly and exited into a darkened visitors' waiting area.

It was about 4:00 A.M. on Sunday morning. I slipped past a few people who were asleep on the couches, and I quietly made my way back to where Sam was. Michael and Gordon were asleep in the two chairs by the bedside. I kissed my fingers and gently touched them to Sam's foot as he continued to sleep under heavy sedation. Not wanting to disturb anyone, I left the ICU and began roaming the quiet, deserted halls of the hospital, nursing the pain in my side with an ice pack I'd gotten from one of the nurses. I continued to experience a cycle of emotions and thoughts—disbelief, shock, grief, emotional pain, and then gratitude. Perhaps it was a combination of lack of sleep, some morphine still in my system, an inability to get a good deep breath, and the piercing pain in my side, but everything just seemed so dreamlike and surreal. I would find a chair or a bench, sit with my head in my hands as I struggled to process what I was going through, then arise and wander some more.

I returned to the waiting room to check on Michael and Sam. As I entered the ICU, I noticed it was almost 8:00 in the morning. Michael was awake, and I asked him if he would like to go to church with me. In my wanderings of the many hospital hallways, I had passed the chapel inside the hospital and noted that there was a church service that would be held that morning. When Michael responded by saying, "Yeah, I really want to go to our church," I realized he wanted to attend the worship service we normally attended, which started at 9:00 A.M. in a building near our home, our ward house.

I knew he was right; we needed to attend church services with our neighbors and friends and not the meeting being held at the hospital. But we had to move quickly if we were to make it on time. I hurried over to Michelle's aunt, Nona Miller, who was in the visitors' waiting area and asked if she would give us a ride home so we could change our clothes and attend our home service. Michelle's parents, Gordon and Audrea, and my parents stayed with Sam while Nona drove Michael and me home.

As we left Primary Children's Medical Center, I knew that the quickest route to our home was 2000 East, past the I-80 underpass, right where the crash had happened. There was another route that she could take to avoid that area altogether, but as we got closer I could tell that Nona was heading on the road that led past the site of the crash. I sat in the backseat, quite emotional about what I might see there and unsure if I was ready to confront that stretch of road yet. The images of that night were still so very fresh and vivid in my mind. As we approached my neighborhood, I leaned forward to ask Nona to take the alternate route. Before I began to speak, I remembered what my father had told me after the accident when I was sixteen.

When the initial investigation of that accident was concluded by the police, I was told to move my car out of the roadway. I would have to drive it only two more blocks to where I worked at LDS Hospital. But while seated in the patrol car, I had resolved that I would never drive a car again, especially that car. I told my father, who had joined me at the accident scene, that I "just couldn't drive that car ever again," and I begged him to drive it for me. Refusing to take the keys that I was trying to press into his hand, he gave me some very wise counsel and encouragement by saying, "When the horse bucks you off, you need to get right back on again." My dad wasn't exactly the equestrian type, and I don't think he had ever been bucked off a horse in his life, but I knew what he meant and that he was right.

● ● ●

I sank back into the seat in Nona's car and sat silently as she drove right past where the tragedy had happened. I was an emotional mess. I had decided I wasn't going to restrict my life

Two little girls leaving flowers and notes at the site of the crash

because of what I was suffering; I knew I would drive that stretch of road again; and, as hard as it might be, I knew I needed to overcome the hesitancy to do so then and there. As we passed the crash site, we saw dozens of bouquets of flowers, stuffed animals, and cards placed on and around the underpass pillars. Taped to the pillar supports were several posters with expressions of sympathy and love for Michelle, Ben, and Anna and our unborn child. I was so impressed and touched by the outpouring of love. I would have missed that had I not been willing to buck up after being bucked off. That was exactly what Michelle had been trying to tell me all those years, that when things get tough you need to take fresh courage and become even more hopeful and confident. That ability came so naturally to her, and I'm sure it was frustrating for her to see me so challenged when it came to life's smaller tests and trials. But I had a chance to show her that those lessons, given over so many years in patience, were starting to have a real effect in her husband's life at a time when they were needed most.

We arrived at our house, and I was again overcome by the scene—neighbors, friends, and family had tied hundreds of ribbons throughout the front yard and up into the large elm tree that stood in front of our home. It was such a beautiful and amazing sight and a wonderful indication of how much Michelle, Ben, and Anna were loved—as well as how much they would be missed.

I don't think either Michael or I had ever changed our clothes faster than that morning. Nona drove us to the chapel and dropped us off outside. Michael and I moved quickly, knowing that the church services had already started. We entered the building and walked toward the middle chapel doors, hoping to find a back row seat to sit in. With the meeting already in progress, I didn't even think about going onto the stand, where I would usually sit as I presided as the bishop over the congregation each week. We stopped just outside the chapel doors, which were propped open. I was amazed to see the chapel full and the overflow area in the cultural hall behind the chapel also filled by the congregation—the church was absolutely packed with people. I felt awkward as people saw Michael and me and as they started alerting others around them. Everyone seemed to be looking toward us in apparent disbelief that we were there.

I tried not to make eye contact with anyone in particular as I still sheepishly looked for a place to sit toward the back. Motioning behind me for Michael to come with me into the overflow area, I began to move forward, when I realized he was no longer behind me.

I looked around for him, but I didn't see him anywhere. I had no idea where he had gone. I didn't know quite what to do as more people began to notice I was there, and I felt increasingly awkward standing there alone. I knew that there were always vacant seats in the front pews, as nobody ever sits in the front benches. I quickly backed out of the overflow area and walked down the hall toward the door that entered into the front of the chapel. I opened it slightly to peer inside without being seen or drawing more attention to myself, and I saw the entire row of church leaders on the stand looking right at me. James Wood was there, and he motioned for me to sit by him on the stand. The last thing I wanted to do by attending the services that morning was to become a spectacle. But as I opened the door fully and entered the chapel, I was overcome by the powerful spirit that I felt. I could hear a collective gasp from the congregation, and I could feel everyone's attention focused on me.

I sat down by James and looked into the congregation and there, seated in the middle of a pew surrounded by all of his friends, was Michael. I again had a powerful assurance that he was going to make it through this trial. As I scanned the congregation, I saw close friends and neighbors, and I felt such a concern for all those who were there seeking peace during such a horrific trial. There was, however, one area of the chapel I did not want to look at that morning. It was the third pew from the pulpit, on the right side of those who sat on the stand. It was where my family had sat for more than six years while I served in various leadership capacities and hadn't been able to sit with them.

My family didn't have to sit in that particular pew. When I had served in other positions and I didn't have to be seated on the stand, Michelle and I preferred to sit in various parts of the chapel each Sunday so we could get to know others better. But while I was occupied on the stand and Michelle was left to tend the children on her own, that pew was close enough to where I sat that if I began to nod off, she quickly dispatched one of the children to come to where I sat and very publicly wake me up. It was also close enough that I could also give any one of them "the look" should they have attention problems of their own. "The look" from me was actually a really big smile, so it wasn't too intimidating, but the children knew it would lead to an unpleasant discussion after church about what I was really smiling about. The only child to really object to sitting so near to me on the stand was Sam who, after it was announced one Sunday that I was presiding at the meeting, scowled, cupped his hands around his mouth, and exclaimed loudly "Boo!" I guess you can't please all the people all the time.

● ● ●

That Sunday, I knew Michelle, Ben, and Anna were there with us, in spirit. Various speakers bore witness of the Savior's grace in their lives. Their witness strengthened my faith so much that by the end of the meeting I wanted to publicly share my recent experiences of that grace and mercy. I arose and declared my personal witness of the plan of happiness and my testimony that because Michelle and I had been married for eternity, I knew I would be with her again. I talked about how Michelle and I would have our children with us as well. I spoke of the Savior's ability to strengthen us to carry our portion of His burden when we take His yoke upon us and learn of Him. That same wonderful enabling grace helped me to speak and witness of Him, way beyond my natural capacity that morning, and especially given the circumstances.

Perhaps of all the people in attendance, the one who most needed that reassurance about the plan of happiness was Michael.

I also saw in the congregation many whom I had encouraged and counseled with as their bishop. There were widows whom I had helped, people struggling in their marriages or with personal challenges, the unemployed and underemployed. There were those who needed encouragement, understanding, and unconditional love, whom I loved and served with all my heart. I told them that Sunday that "if your testimonies of Jesus Christ are not strong enough, or if you need to lean on the witness of someone else for a time, I invite you to lean on my witness that the Savior lives." I assured them that "my testimony was strong enough for both of us, because I know that He lives and has prepared a way for all of us to be together in heaven again."

I sat down in awe of the strength of that witness—again I was on the Lord's errand, and He had given me a message to be delivered and the power to deliver it. My declaration of the Savior was stronger and surer than it had ever been. After the meeting, James drove Michael and me back to our home. We quickly changed our clothes, and Nona, who had been waiting for us at the house, took us back to the hospital to be with Sam. She again took the route through the crash site. This time, however, there was no hesitation or dread on my part. I knew it was the right road to take so I could again see the sweet expressions of love and sympathy that had been placed there. What a wonderful opportunity to again quietly express my gratitude in prayer for being blessed with so much.

●　●　●

9

Eternal Self-Preservation

That evening as Michael and I sat at Sam's bedside, we were visited by a couple of senior authorities of The Church of Jesus Christ of Latter-day Saints. The weekend prior to the crash, these two brethren had been the visiting authorities for a gathering of several congregations, called a stake conference, that Michelle and I were involved with. Their schedules permitted them to pay us a visit in the hospital that Sunday night to minister to my family. They first wanted to give Sam a blessing, and again we were assured that he would be healed. It was comforting to know we were all getting the same inspiration regarding Samuel.

One of the Church leaders then turned to me and said, "Now let's give you a blessing." I was blessed with the strength to carry on and was wisely advised that time would be a healing balm. It was a sweet gesture on their part of service, love, and support.

As they left, I thought of my local Church leaders and of the charity and service they had shown to my family through the years. They had dedicated their time to serving so many without

Remembrances left by family and friends at the Williams's home

pay, and I had regularly drawn strength from them. I thought of my assistants in my ministry—my bishopric counselors, Michael Hennessy and Ron Jessee—and their families, and all of the other families in the congregation who worked so tirelessly in such equally loving and charitable ways. I also thought of those brethren who specifically watched over my family on a monthly basis, our home teachers. The visits and blessings they had given as my children grew were just as powerful as those that were pronounced on Sam, Michael, and me that day. My appreciation and gratitude grew for dedicated disciples of Jesus Christ who were always willing to make time to bless my family. It was a gentle reminder that these were all evidences and expressions of love from the Savior, who is the fount of charity, mercy, kindness, and long-suffering, and that it didn't really matter which vessel that power flowed through. What mattered was the source of that power—the Savior himself—and our willingness to let his light shine through us, illuminating the lives of others.

I spent the remainder of the evening by Sam's side. Not as many visitors came that night; however, a dear friend flew in from Phoenix to be with me. I was very touched by that gesture. His presence provided a great deal of support and strength to me throughout the evening. Later that night, I again made my way to the small room by the visitors' lounge, yearning to vocally converse with my Father in Heaven in prayer. I entered the room, closed the door, and knelt down by the side of the bed, leaving the lights on. I wept as I began to express my gratitude for the many wonderful blessings I had been given in my life. As I prayed and pondered about what I was experiencing, a verse of scripture came forcefully into my mind: "Forgive, and ye shall be forgiven" (Luke 6:37).

As that verse repeated itself in my mind, I could see that the "forgiveness" I had offered, that I had been commanded to offer, could more accurately be described as a plea for mercy and love that I was commanded to extend, allowing the Savior to take my burden when I "let it go." It was a command to love God and exercise faith in Him and to love my neighbor, thereby obeying the two great commandments. At my lowest point while still inside the car, when I felt as if my soul was being crushed, I pleaded for the Savior's mercy and for His deliverance. When I heard the circumstances regarding who had caused this accident, I again pleaded for the Savior's mercy. When I was so alone and in such pain, I was delivered by the Savior's mercy and love. I couldn't allow myself to ever go back on that commitment to forgive. In the days of grieving that I knew yet lay ahead, I knew that decision would be tested, and I needed to be prepared to stand strong.

I also understood why in another verse of scripture the Savior warns those who don't forgive: "But if ye do not forgive, neither will your Father which is in heaven forgive your trespasses" (Mark 11:26). From my Bible study, I knew the Savior was frequently derided by the Pharisees and Sadducees for exercising His authority to forgive sins, and yet the Savior *is* the only one who is authorized to forgive sin. I finished my prayer grateful that I had been spared the temptation to think that forgiveness was mine to give or withhold, or that it was in any way linked to whether I thought someone did or did not merit forgiveness by his or her remorse or lack thereof. My much publicized "act of forgiveness" was truly borne of my great weakness, my own nothingness, and my desire for eternal self-preservation so that I didn't stand condemned before God. I had to do unto others as I wanted the Savior to do unto me. I wanted His mercy to cleave unto any mercy I could extend, so that at the end of my life my sins could be covered by the cloak of the Savior's mercy, and I would be found completely clean. If I didn't extend mercy without reservation, it would be difficult to have it extended to me, and I could be fully exposed to the punishment of that greater sin of assigning a power to myself that is not mine, resisting and perhaps even fighting the Savior's mercy and heading for a truly miserable state of suffering.

I awoke and found that I had fallen asleep on my knees. I stood up and walked out of the room into the visitors' area, heartened to see that it was 5:00 A.M. and that I had finally been able to get a few hours of sleep.

· · ·

IO

Forgiving Hearts

The media interest in my family's tragedy coupled with the expression of unconditional forgiveness had grown fairly intense. My stake president, James Wood, acted as the public spokesman for my family, fielding the many requests from the media for information about me, Michael, and Sam. The requests quickly intensified as interest in the story grew. The press wanted to know if I had any additional statements that I would make, beyond what had already been reported. I was so focused on Michael and Sam that I didn't want to think about anything else, but the requests didn't stop. On Monday morning we determined that the best way to address the various media requests would be to organize a press conference. James worked with the public affairs department of the LDS Church to schedule a press conference at a church building in my neighborhood for that afternoon at two.

I didn't give the event another thought until 1:00 P.M. when my father said, "We had better go to the house to change clothes so we can make it to the press conference on time." Panic set in when I realized I had one hour to get home, change, and prepare something to say in front of the cameras and reporters. We hurriedly left the hospital, and I sat in the backseat of my parents' car as my mother and father drove me home. As we exited the hospital parking garage, I asked my mother for a pad and pencil and began to quickly write down some thoughts in a hurried attempt to come up with some kind of semi-intelligent statement to make. The closer we got to my home, the more I panicked. As we pulled into my driveway, I still didn't have any cohesive thoughts written down, just some words that had been crossed out and a few incomplete sentences about Michelle, Ben, and Anna.

James was already at my house waiting for me. I changed into a suit and went downstairs to my computer. It was almost 2:00 P.M. I turned on the computer and said a prayer asking that whatever I said could be a help and a blessing to others. As soon as my fingers started typing, I immediately knew what I had to write, and it wasn't anything that I had prepared on the way to the house. It was a short and simple expression of what the Savior wanted me to say based on what I had been taught the previous night and early that morning in prayer. I hit the print button, grabbed the "press statement," and ran back upstairs.

We drove to the meetinghouse and entered through a rear door to meet briefly with the public affairs representative who had organized the press conference. We said a prayer together and walked toward the front of the building. No suggestions of what to say were offered. The prayer for heavenly help filled me with a great deal of confidence that I would know what to say in the moment I needed to say it. As we moved toward the front of the building where the media was, I suddenly felt as if we were joined by hundreds of unseen individuals who were also walking with me. I couldn't believe the power that I felt surround me as we

Chris speaking to the press, February 12, 2007

proceeded down the hall. We exited the building, and I stepped up to the microphones. I thanked the reporters for coming while I opened up the sheet of paper I had been prompted to type, and read the following:

This truly is a bitter cup that my family has been asked to partake of, but with such a miraculous outpouring of love and prayer from the community, I know that it will all be all right one day.

On behalf of my sweet wife, our children, and my extended family, we would invite you if you are in a position to extend a single act of kindness, a token of mercy, or an expression of forgiveness, would you do it by Valentine's Day and then, if you feel to so do, write that experience down and share it with my two surviving boys by sending it to the address that the radio and TV outlets will provide. I can think of no greater valentine that you could give to someone, or that my sons and I could present to my sweetheart, than that.

May God bless every individual one of you for your goodness, thank you.

By then I felt as if there were indeed a thousand hands at my back, supporting and sustaining me through that experience. Only sixty-five hours had elapsed since the tragic crash and deaths of my wife and two of my children—an impact that had ripped through my family and the community. And as I stood before the local media, I felt such sustaining support as I tried to convey with conviction what I believe the Savior wanted me to say in that public situation. In the face of tragedy, there was a call for mercy and love and an invitation to exercise greater faith in Him by inviting those who have suffered, however unjustly, to lay their burdens at the feet of the Savior and let them go. My privilege was to have a front-row seat, watching the Master Himself teaching, preaching, and healing. As I read the statement, I was also so impressed with the Savior's use of the Valentine's holiday—usually a time for giving hearts to those we love—to invite the world to give the heart that would endure eternally, a heart filled with mercy, a heart desiring kindness, and a heart of empowering forgiveness and hope of a better day.

I am not that articulate or wise to have come up with that type of statement by myself; I truly am nothing. I know better than anyone where the true source of that power came from as I stood before the microphones, that it was the grace of the Savior that had enabled me to accept this invitation to extend mercy and forgiveness. I was simply a witness for the peace and immediate healing that comes from "letting it go." I sincerely hoped that others would be inspired to cast off the burdens they were carrying, pleading for greater faith in Jesus Christ to enjoy an added measure of His peace and mercy in their lives.

I had been advised that there might be some questions after the statement was read, but I thought that I would at most be asked a few easy, simple questions and that would be it. As soon as I finished reading the statement, all of the reporters started questioning me at once. For a fraction of a second I panicked, realizing this could be a bit of a grilling, and I knew that I was not that quick on my feet, and there was no easy escape. But as I began to answer the questions, I realized what all the hands at my back were there for. With each question, especially those dealing with my wife and children, I felt an incredible amount of strength to remain poised and to know exactly what I needed to say in response. I'm quite sure that when the heavenly hosts heard it was Chris Williams who would be speaking at the press conference, multiple celestial emergency alarms sounded, and a large number of angels were sent with the express direction to "get down there and make sure he doesn't say anything stupid!"

I was asked about forgiveness and what I thought that should mean by way of consequence; did I intend for there to be no penalty? I replied, "Although there is power in forgiveness, it does not relieve us of consequences." It was a fascinating experience to hear my mouth declaratively state a truth while my mind was racing for a response.

As I spoke of my family, I wondered if one of those hands at my back was that of Michelle. Whether that was actually the case, I don't know, but feeling that she may be aware of what was transpiring, or at the very least listening in, I wanted to use that as an opportunity to publicly pay a tribute to her. In a response to one of the questions about the offered forgiveness, I said, "After being married to such a wonderful woman and incredible example to me for eighteen and a half years, my willingness to follow the Savior and forgive was also my chance to show her that I really had been listening to and learning from her all those years." I really wasn't trying to idealize my spouse while debasing myself because of our separation; it was borne of my recent recollection of some experiences with Michelle where I had really tried her patience.

One such example of what she had to put up with occurred in the spring of 2004. Michelle had suggested that we take a trip to New York and visit the Susquehanna River, an important historical site for the LDS Church. We planned a trip that included several days in Manhattan, then a drive through Pennsylvania past the Susquehanna River monument, and on to Palmyra to see other LDS Church historical sites, ending our trip with a visit to Niagara Falls.

After a wonderful time in Manhattan as a family, we rented a car and started our journey through Pennsylvania to Palmyra. By the time we hit the bridge over the Susquehanna River, seven miles from the commemoration site, it was much later in the day than I had planned. I decided, without consulting Michelle, to keep driving toward Palmyra so we wouldn't arrive in the middle of the night. As we went over the bridge, I looked at Michelle, pointed to the river, said, "Well, there's the Susquehanna River," and barreled on toward Palmyra. I figured if Michelle really wanted to stop and see the monument, she would have said so.

The next morning in Palmyra we left our hotel room and visited the Joseph Smith family farm. A very pleasant missionary couple greeted us at the visitors' center and began telling us about some things that we could see that morning. Michelle, noting that something had been omitted from the list, asked, "Where is the Susquehanna River?"

The man, a bit bewildered, answered, "It's about two hundred miles that-a-way," and he gestured in a vague southerly direction.

Michelle, realizing what I had done, turned to me with "that look." If looks could really kill, I and anyone standing behind me for miles would have been dead instantly

In an effort to salvage the situation, I think I said something like, "Well, we could just drive there this afternoon and then come back." I then learned another valuable life lesson: throwing gas on a fire will not put it out. The unfortunate truth is that I was really mad because I knew she was right. I was pretty inconsiderate of her feelings, and that wasn't easy to admit. She quickly resigned herself to our situation; we weren't going to see the place that provided the initial inspiration for coming on the trip.

Michelle and the children had a great day at the Smith family farm and the other historical sites around Palmyra. I spent the day being taken to the Smith family woodshed by the Holy Spirit, so to speak; I kicked myself for being so selfish. Later that afternoon, after having been chastened and humbled throughout the day, I begged Michelle's forgiveness. She was honestly surprised to find I had been thinking about it all day; she had let it go immediately. As we stood atop the Hill Cumorah where Joseph Smith had received a great treasure—the plates of gold that contained the writings of followers of Jesus Christ who lived on this hemisphere—I said something about the treasure she was in my life. She wasn't much for cornball sentimentality, but she knew I was trying to say I loved her very much. Apology accepted.

● ● ●

As I stood before the media answering their questions, I felt I owed it to Michelle, who was observing her husband from a different vantage point, to show her that I had learned a great deal from her.

The press conference ended, and we returned to the church building. In my statement I had referenced the "bitter cup" that my family was partaking of, and as we walked through the building to return to our car, I was reminded that the Savior didn't drink it all at once, that He drank it over time until it was all gone. That was a merciful reassurance that I didn't have to take this portion all at once either, that I could press on with each sip as I had strength to do it.

●●●

II

Heaven Won't Be
Heaven Without . . .

My dad drove my mom and me back to the hospital to be
with Sam and Michael. Michelle and I had always reserved
Monday evenings as a night for our family to gather together, but
I hadn't made any plans or prepared anything for that particular
Monday night. Even though we were now an earthly family of
three, I wanted to keep that commitment to hold that weekly
family meeting. I arranged for us to use a conference room close
to the children's ICU where Sam was located, and I invited the
extended family, as well as the families of my counselors, the
Hennessys and Jessees. As I was planning out the agenda for that
unique family night, I was interrupted by one of the hospital staff
wondering if I would take a phone call from *LDS Church News.*
Had it been any other news magazine or media outlet, I would
have said no without hesitation, but I really liked the *Church
News,* so I said that I would be happy to take the call.

Gerry Avant introduced herself as an editor of the *Church
News.* Somehow she had not been contacted about the press

conference and had missed it, and she was wondering if she could meet with me that afternoon at the hospital to conduct her own interview. I thought it was funny that the LDS Church public affairs had arranged the meeting but that the editor of the *LDS Church News* had not gotten the press conference e-mail. Like so many things in life that appear coincidental, it would soon become apparent why that particular oversight had occurred.

Gerry and I met in a small room just outside of the ICU an hour before our family meeting was going to begin. I once again felt the room fill with unseen strength and felt the Holy Spirit inspiring me with answers to her questions that were way beyond my natural abilities. We talked of the forgiveness that had been extended, and I told her, "As a disciple of Christ, I had no other choice," summing up what I had felt during my conversation with my Heavenly Father. I continued by saying that I wanted to make sure that I would live in such a way that I'd have the right to be with my family for eternity. Then I finished by summarizing what the last seventy-two hours had come to mean, that the last thing I wanted to do the moment I realized that my wife and children had passed to the other side was to break a commandment; as a disciple of Christ, I had no other choice but to forgive.

We then talked about the "bitter cup" my family had been given. After the press conference, I had wanted to clarify that in no way was I trying to compare myself to the Savior, and I was not trying to be sacrilegious in any way. But the analogy was intended to explain, as I understood it, that because of the way the Savior went through his tremendous trial, here in my miniscule, incomparable challenge, I could take hope. I remember telling her that in the Garden of Gethsemane, the Savior drank of it a little, and then He went back to His disciples, to His friends, for a little bit of support, and then He drank some more. He had an angel come and strengthen Him and support Him, and He drank a little more. He went back to His disciples, and was able to have a little bit of a respite. Then He drank the remainder on the cross, until it was all gone, until it was finished. I finished my explanation of the bitter cup by saying that I felt it was like our lives; we're not asked to drink more than we're able to all at once. I then told her that I knew one day all the pain and suffering would be gone, leaving only the joy of having passed through it successfully, but only if I remained faithful to the end.

By that time I had been informed that the name of the teenager was Cameron White. When I began to talk to Gerry about Cameron, I started to marvel at what I was saying. Of that conversation, Gerry wrote:

> *To his ward members and during the news interview [Bishop Williams] bore powerful testimony of the Atonement. He said that he wants to be among the friends who will visit the young man "for however long it takes" for him to recover from his role in the tragedy. "My wife and my two children are taken care of," he said. "They're in a place of rest, a place of peace—Paradise, as it's been named. The true tragedy of this event, the eternal tragedy, would be if this young man chose not to partake of the Atonement, and if we lost that soul. It's one thing to lose a life, but in the resurrection and eternal families, that can be healed through the love of our Savior. This can be an experience of growth, an experience where one day we're very grateful that we were able to pass through it. But if we were to lose that soul, for me, personally, heaven just wouldn't be heaven. I don't know if I could feel celestial joy knowing that there was a soul lost*

because of this accident" (Gerry Avant, "Forgiveness is the only option," LDS Church News, *February 17, 2007).*

As I spoke to her about those eternal truths regarding the great worth of a soul in the sight of God, I felt the immense, personal love the Savior had for Cameron. I had felt of Christ's mercy, I had felt of His concern, and I had heard the call for forgiveness, mercy, and healing, but I had not thought of the earnest desire He had for His son Cameron White to come home. As I spoke of Cameron, he was no longer "the teenage boy that had caused this to happen," he became Cameron White, my brother.

I again reminded myself that I, too, was a sinner and that if I hoped to lay claim to mercy and be forgiven by the only person able to truly forgive sin, I needed to be willing to extend mercy to someone whose choices had been so devastating to my family. To claim mercy, I truly did need to be willing to extend it. This point was so forcefully and powerfully emphasized when, later in the week, I had the chance to view Benjamin prior to the funeral.

I had been told by the mortuary that we might not want to have Benjamin's casket open at the viewing, given the injuries he had sustained. The mortuary did the very best they could, but when I saw Ben, I was overcome with the damage that his body had sustained. My sweet, caring Benjamin had literally been crushed by the impact. As haunting and difficult as that image is to recall, even to this day, I have since then continually expressed great gratitude to my Father in Heaven for allowing *His* son to be bruised and broken that we all could be healed.

Perhaps I had been uniquely prepared for that perspective on Ben's injuries years earlier as a missionary learning the Spanish language in the Missionary Training Center in Provo, Utah.

While there, I remember seeing a movie depicting the story of a drawbridge keeper who opened a bridge for ships to pass through and lowered it for trains to pass over (*The Bridge*, 1978, produced and directed by Robert N. Hatch).

In the movie, a large passenger train approaches the bridge, and the man begins to lock the drawbridge into place; however, the mechanisms don't lock as they should, and he has to run to a lever by the tracks to manually hold the drawbridge closed. As the train approaches, he sees his young son running toward him from the far side of the bridge, calling, "Daddy, where are you?" The father desperately yells for his son to go back and get off the tracks, but his son doesn't hear him over the noise of the oncoming train. The father releases the lever for a moment in order to run and warn his son, but realizes that the train is too close; he'll never be able grab his son and make it back in time to hold the drawbridge lever in place so the train can pass safely. With an agonizing cry, he grasps the lever and holds on as the train speeds past him. The passengers on the train are unaware of the child who has been hit or of the sobbing man, still hanging onto the lever long after the train is out of sight.

When I saw that movie, and I realized more profoundly than I ever had before what my Father in Heaven may have endured while His son suffered, I was physically overcome. I became faint and had to lie down on a row of chairs. I was moved by the powerful witness I felt of the love my Father in Heaven has for me and what He allowed His Son to pass through on my behalf, something I had either not considered before or had thought about too casually.

• • •

At the end of the interview with Gerry, I again mentioned how funny I thought it was that the *LDS Church News* had been left off the e-mail notice sent about the press conference. Making light of the oversight, I asked her, "You are on speaking terms, aren't you?" Gerry laughed and again remarked that it had never happened before, but then she paused. She inquired about the accident I had when I was sixteen years old.

I explained to Gerry that as soon as I obtained my driver's license I got a job as a surgical orderly at the busiest hospital in the city, then LDS Hospital on the steep northern hills of Salt Lake City. I transported patients to and from surgery, obtained supplies during surgery as needed, and cleaned and prepared surgical rooms between surgeries. It was a very responsible position for a sixteen year old, especially when the alternative job opportunities for someone that age were usually flipping burgers or bussing tables. The work was fascinating, and I would try to be assigned to the rooms where some of the more intriguing surgeries were being performed.

On my way to work one day, just months after starting the job and only two blocks from the hospital, I was stunned by the sound of a very loud bang on the front of my car. I immediately slammed on the brakes, not knowing what had happened. My mind raced to make sense of what I had just heard. As there were no other cars around, I initially thought someone had thrown a large rock at my car. I looked around to see who was in the area and, in the rearview mirror, I saw a little boy standing in the street where I had just passed.

When the image of the boy in the road connected in my mind with the loud noise I had heard, I realized I had just hit him with my car. I quickly got out and ran back to where he stood. He was alert and wasn't crying, and I couldn't see any signs of injury. I checked for any cuts or bleeding, repeatedly asking him if he was okay. Neighbors rushed toward us to assist, and I was told that help was on the way. Ambulances and fire trucks quickly arrived, and a policeman placed me in the back of a police car while they investigated the accident. I was in shock, but I felt comforted by my observation that the young boy looked unhurt; he was not crying, and he was responsive to questions. Given the right medical attention, I was sure he would be fine.

I continued to sit in the police car all alone, struggling to understand how I had hit a small boy with my car. I had never even seen him come into the street. As I sat, I could see more emergency and hospital personnel converging around my car a hundred feet in front of me.

It seemed as though I had been in that patrol car for an eternity—in disbelief of what was transpiring and wondering why this was happening to me. I had been going less than the posted twenty-five-mile-an-hour speed limit, I wasn't under the influence of anything, nor had I been distracted in any way. I had simply been trying to drive to my new job.

A tow truck arrived, and the front of my car was raised, yet they never hauled the car away. It remained there with the front end suspended while many people worked around it. As I sat alone in the police car in a fog of shock and numbness, struggling to make sense of what I was seeing before me, the silence inside the car was interrupted by an officer opening the door. He sat in the front seat and asked me again for the details of what had happened. I recounted exactly what I could recall and answered his subsequent questions with as much exactness as I possibly could. He told me to remain in the car and they would get back to me, but I stopped him as he was leaving by asking, "What are they doing with my car?"

He turned back toward me and said, "There's a boy trapped in the wheel well of your car, and we're trying to get him out."

He then grabbed his clipboard and exited the patrol car. The loud bang of the door closing left me in silence, and I was again left alone, so terribly alone. I didn't move. I didn't know how to think; I just stared at the scene before me.

• • •

I knew that the boy's name was Jimmy Forster, the son of John and Sue Forster, but I told Gerry that I never met with them after the accident and didn't know what had happened to them since. Gerry then told me that John had worked with her at the *LDS Church News* more than twenty years previous, and she remembered him talking about the accident. From her recollection, the Forsters' sons had been playfully chasing each other around their front yard. The chase eventually led between two parked cars and into the street, directly into the path of my vehicle, the five-year-old boy striking the right front of my vehicle and the three-year-old boy emerging into the street shortly afterward.

I told Gerry how hard it had been for me in the days following the accident. I prayed for and pleaded with Heavenly Father that Jimmy would survive, that somehow miraculously he would live, only to receive the news a few days after the accident that Jimmy had passed away.

Shortly after Jimmy's funeral, I received a letter from the Forsters. Jimmy's mother, Sue, wrote, "We know you, Chris, were chosen to create the physical change in Jimmy to allow him to leave us as the world understands death." She continued, "Because of the physical damage, it made it much easier for us to let him go. . . . Take courage, Chris, and lean on your testimony, all that you've learned of God IS true, now let it comfort you and allow you to work for Him in every other way he has in store for you." Those were inspired and marvelous words of comfort written by an incredible woman who was herself grieving the separation from her son.

I explained to Gerry that for years I privately struggled for an answer about that tragic experience. Why did I have to endure that trial at such a young age? What was I to learn from it? I said there was no immediate answer from the Lord, just years of pondering and reflecting on that trial without a significant resolution.

I then told her that in 2006, more than twenty years after the accident and one week before I was to deliver my first sermon as a newly called bishop, I was awakened very early in the morning with a strong impression that I needed to write in detail about that tragedy I endured as a sixteen-year-old. I went into the kitchen, got a notebook, and began to write. I had never before written anything about what I had gone through; I had never really talked about it to anyone, not even much to Michelle. I had just buried it, hoping it would fade away with the passage of time. But as I sat at the kitchen table in the early hours of that morning, I could remember it in great detail. Through tear-filled eyes I wrote what that experience meant to me. I was given an opportunity to turn around, look back into the past, and see how the Lord used that tragic accident to show me my weakness so I could be humbled.

I could see that in the months following Jimmy's death I began to make choices that would strengthen my relationship with my Savior, that would help me surrender my petty will for a better way. Slowly I changed as the Lord changed me. I pushed myself out of my comfort zone and tried to use the abilities I had been blessed with. As an example, I didn't enjoy singing in public. I'm not sure many teenagers do, but people had remarked at various times in my youth that I had a nice voice. Thinking I might have some ability to sing, and in an effort to stay true to my commitment to not bury any talent, I tried out for every singing group that my high school sponsored and was accepted into every one. I participated in as many diverse activities as I possibly could to refine whatever talent I might have. I ran for student body president and lost, and then I "got back on the horse" and ran for senior class president and won. (Had I known then of the reunions I would subsequently be in charge of, I would probably have let someone else have the pleasure of taking the reins and riding that horse. Live and learn, I guess.) I tried out for and received parts in the school musical and school play; I joined science and academic clubs. I joined the school paper staff and wrote for the sports section, took advanced placement courses to further push myself, performed a piano concerto with the school orchestra, and tried to know and be a friend to everyone at school.

I didn't list those accomplishments to Gerry to brag or boast because, truthfully, I wasn't that good at any of them. But I told her that as I looked back into my past and wrote about that accident, with a perspective those twenty-plus years provided, I could see what I had allowed the Lord to make of my life because of what I experienced. I could stop wondering, *Why was this allowed to happen to me at such a young age?*, and instead I could start detailing what Christ was able to make of my life and who He was able to bless through me because that accident was allowed to happen. In the years after the accident, Sue Forster's words were realized in my life; I was blessed to refine myself further to "work for Him in every way He has in store" for me.

● ● ●

Gerry proceeded to tell me what had happened to the Forsters after their son passed away. She gave me John's phone number, and I called him several weeks later. He told me that his family had been thinking of me, too, through those many years. It was wonderful to finally make his acquaintance over the phone. I had never felt that I needed to be forgiven for what had happened, as I knew Jimmy's death had been completely accidental, but I was able to talk with him from a point of mutual perspective; I too knew what it was like to lose a son.

For more than twenty years I had thought of and prayed for the Forsters, and after talking with Gerry at Primary Children's Medical Center and having experienced another terrible tragedy in my life, I was getting that final piece of the story to bring the first major trial in my life to closure. I could view the past with a confidence to declare, "I endured it well," and with a greater surety that I could endure this trial too.

I thanked Gerry for the amazing blessing it was for me to speak with her. We both knew that it was no oversight, coincidence, or accident that her name was omitted from the press conference list.

I left her and entered the conference room where Michael and the rest of our family and friends were gathered for our family night. It was a very special and memorable family meeting as we talked of the reality of eternal families. As we ended the meeting with a family prayer, feeling a vast sense of comfort and peace together, we were unaware of the terrible events that were unfolding at a shopping mall a few miles away and the need the entire city of Salt Lake would soon have for the Savior's message of healing and peace.

$\bullet \ \bullet \ \bullet$

12

Piercing Tragedy with Love

My sleep was still measured in minutes, not hours. In the middle of the night and again early in the morning, I walked the quiet, mostly empty halls of Primary Children's Medical Center seeking solace. It was Tuesday, February 13, 2007. I had wandered to the cafeteria to find something to eat when a large, bold newspaper headline in a vending machine caught my eye. It read "Mall massacre." Another byline declared "Trolley Square: Emotionless killer gunned down victims randomly." I couldn't believe what I was reading. My knees gave way, and I sunk onto a bench, staring at the headline through tears of emotion and sadness. I felt as if the whole world was imploding. Life was already surreal enough, but to read that five people had just been murdered was almost too much to endure.

I finally arose from the bench and purchased the paper. As I unfolded it, a headline on the lower section of the front page caught my eye: "Crash victim issues a call for forgiveness." Senseless tragedies can harden the heart and tempt us to lose faith in the world,

DESERET
Morning News
VOL. 157/NO. 244
TUESDAY, FEBRUARY 13, 2007
SALT LAKE CITY, UTAH

Mall massacre

■ Gunman at Trolley Square kills 5, wounds others before he's slain

By Ben Winslow, Pat Reavy
and Wendy Leonard
Deseret Morning News

A man went on a shooting rampage inside the Trolley Square mall, killing five people and wounding numerous others before dying in a shootout with police.

Trolley Square shooting

1. Victim dead in west parking lot
2. One person hit near Rasul Rock Cafe
3. Police command post
4. Shooter killed in hallway by Cabin Fever
5. One person hit at Tabula Rasa
6. Shots fired at Spaghetti Factory
7. One person hit in front of Williams-Sonoma

SOURCE: Salt Lake City Police scanner traffic

Eyewitnesses said the man first began shooting outside the mall at about 6:45 p.m. Monday, near the parking terrace.

"He was in the west parking lot; he came out from underneath. I looked and I said, 'That guy has a gun!'" said Ron Matson, who was sitting by the windows of the Desert Edge Brewery. "I saw him pump and shoot a couple of rounds when he's coming from the parking lot into the building."

Inside the mall, chaos erupted.

"I saw a guy run in the hallway in front

Please see **SHOOTINGS** *on A10*

A Salt Lake City police officer squats, his gun drawn, next to a shooting victim inside the Trolley Square Mall, Monday night.

MIKE TERRY, DESERET MORNING NEWS

Crash victim issues a call for forgiveness

By Pat Reavy
Deseret Morning News

As Christopher Williams was being extricated from his overturned SUV onto a backboard to be taken to the hospital, he looked over at his vehicle and the car that had just crashed into him, killing his pregnant wife and two of his children.

It was at that moment Williams said he had a decision to make. That decision, he said, was to "unconditionally forgive" the person who had just caused the accident. By forgiving, Williams said the healing process could continue without being "hampered by another step."

Monday, Williams showed the great composure some had already seen since Friday night's accident as he addressed the media for the first time.

Friday's accident on 2000 East near 2700 South claimed the lives of his 41-year-old wife, Michelle, who

Please see **WILLIAMS** *on A8*

Christopher Williams speaks to the media Monday about the death of his pregnant wife and two children. He said he learned the power of forgiveness from his wife. "This is what she would want to do," he said of forgiving the teen driver.

AUGUST MILLER, DESERET MORNING NEWS

Deseret Morning News front page excerpts, February 13, 2007,
articles on Trolley Square tragedy and Chris's press conference

but the Savior's challenge issued through me to actively combat and fight those temptations with acts of kindness and mercy, and to do so by Valentine's Day, seemed more timely than ever.

• • •

When I made the initial request at the press conference, I had no idea of the responses that simple challenge would create. I would eventually receive thousands of letters and e-mails from all over the world describing acts of kindness, mercy, and charity that were offered. Many included expressions of love, reconciliation, and newly offered forgiveness. There were stories of loss and abuse, of people enduring terrible offenses. Some found peace through "letting it go," and others indicated that while they were still struggling, they had a new perspective on their situation and felt increased hope and faith. I could see in my mind's eye people letting go of their burdens by placing them in the Savior's care. They were putting on the defensive armor of God and carrying, as their only weapon, a sword representing the word of God, and that word was Love, unconditionally extended out, piercing misery.

There were similar themes that ran through the letters. Many of the parents indicated a desire to be more patient and loving with their children. Spouses wrote of how they wanted to love and serve their companions, letting go of the offenses they felt they had received. Hundreds contained this line of reasoning: "If you can forgive someone for doing that to your family, certainly I can forgive," and then they would describe to me what they were newly committing to let go of.

Many of the notes and e-mails came from children, some obviously assisted by their parents. Hundreds of e-mails said things such as "I sent some cookies to my neighbors because one doesn't have a family and it makes me feel good," or "Today my friend just came back from being sick, so I wrote a valentine card that said 'we missed you very much.'" Others were commitments by children to serve others: "I will help anyone that is sad, I will help them anyway I can," and "I will be nice to everyone." One boy saw that the lunch lady at school was "a little grumpy" and thought she could use a valentine, so he brought her a special homemade valentine's card.

Many families dedicated a day of service, offered in honor of Michelle, Ben, and Anna. One family in San Francisco wrote how they spent a day serving others, distributing coats and clothing to the homeless on the streets, taking toys to the children at a shelter for abused women and children, and providing business suits for the women to use in job interviews. Many wrote how they found the experience so rewarding they decided to make service a family tradition every Valentine's Day.

Several hundred of those e-mails and letters actually arrived by Valentine's Day, and they were a welcome reprieve from the rest of my Valentine's Day activities as we began to prepare for a funeral. I knew that my wife's obituary would be the last Valentine's Day card that I would write for her, and I wanted it to be something she would appreciate. I wrote that "she exhibited great faith in finally agreeing to marry Chris after several years of courtship" and that "after over eighteen years of continued courtship after marriage, Chris had the privilege of hearing Michelle recently admit that she had made the right choice."

That sweet moment came on a trip Michelle and I made to Chicago just months before the crash. For years she had wanted to see lightning bugs or fireflies. We had made a trip to Nauvoo thinking that the timing of the trip would allow us to see some there, but we didn't see any; it was too late and too cold in the season.

Then for her fortieth birthday, I secretly purchased a firefly kit similar to those used at the Pirates of the Caribbean ride at Disneyland, a familiar site to those who have floated through that bayou scene at the beginning of the ride. I spent the entire night before her birthday installing that kit throughout the backyard. The next evening during her birthday party, when it was dark enough, I excitedly plugged in the fireflies for her enjoyment. We watched as the lights, powered by small fans, danced in the dark, simulating the look of lightning bugs. She was so thankful for the gesture and really enjoyed the addition to the backyard, but I knew at the end of the night that only the real thing would suffice.

Finally, while on our trip to Chicago, she got her wish. We were strolling along the lakefront trail one evening when, to our surprise, we saw a single, solitary firefly in the air. We followed it for a quarter mile as it flew from the vicinity of Grant Park to the mouth of the Chicago River. She was so thrilled that she had finally seen a real firefly and, as she expressed it, grateful for a husband who allowed her to realize the desires of her heart.

• • •

Michelle was easy to love and serve because she just loved life. In her obituary we tried to capture the way she lived her life when we wrote that "she loved fireworks, fireflies, falling stars, holidays, celebrations, decorations, photos, and so much more."

As I pondered how united Michelle and I had become over time, I realized that this Valentine's Day, February 14, 2007, was maybe the best one we had shared together, because she knew, better than I had ever been able to express to her before, by virtue of her new vantage point, the love I had for her, and I could feel through the Spirit the love she had for me.

● ● ●

13

A Misery Avoided

I had hoped and prayed that Sam would heal well enough to be able to attend the funeral. I wanted both of my sons with me so we could pass through that trial together. Because of the head trauma Sam had suffered, evidenced by the bleeding he had in his brain, when he finally was allowed to "awake" earlier in the week, we found that he had no idea what was going on. Being familiar with computers, the only thing I could relate it to was a computer needing a hard reset, being totally rebooted. Sam had to relearn everything—how to eat, how to walk, how to speak, all the while working through a formidable amount of confusion.

During that week, I worked with him in physical therapy, helping him remember words, work on simple puzzles, and go up and down a few stairs. He was nourished through a feeding tube while he relearned how to eat on his own. However, I knew we couldn't delay the funeral further, and after consulting together as a family, we decided to make arrangements for friends and family to be with Sam in the hospital during the viewing and funeral. I knew he would be healed, but I again had to allow that miracle to happen in the Lord's way and time.

We held the viewing on Friday night, February 16. After a week of such powerful emotional contradictions, I was just about spent. I didn't know how I was going to get through a viewing and a funeral. Once again I had the privilege of relying on the Savior's enabling power to allow me to pass gracefully through a very difficult experience I couldn't complete on my own. We arrived at the funeral home about an hour before the viewing was to start. It was the first time I had seen my wife and children since our good-byes in the car. It was then that I realized how much Michelle and Ben had been physically crushed.

Earlier in the week Michelle's mother, Audrea, and her Aunt Nona had dressed Michelle's body for burial. I had been invited to assist with that somber task, but I just couldn't do it. As I looked at Michelle, Anna, and Ben in the caskets, the sadness and the strength I experienced in the car during my first viewing came rushing back. Michael and I shared a profound moment of mourning before the visitors arrived as we sat together close to the caskets and hugged each other, looking through tears on the rest of our family. We both felt the strength, the hands at our backs, supporting us through the entire evening.

The funeral was held Saturday, February 17. I had prayed for the same strength to make it through that day that I had felt the previous evening. *How else could I bury my wife and children?* I thought. As we drove to the chapel where the funeral was to be held, I was relieved that it was such a temperate, beautiful day. The middle of February could have brought snow, bitter cold, or a depressing, pollution-fueled inversion, yet on this particular mid-February day we were blessed with great weather under a clear, light blue sky.

In the church building, prior to the funeral services, our entire extended family gathered around the three open caskets. In my prayers the previous evening I thought of how I had somehow failed in my desire to never let anything happen to Michelle, and how I had somehow failed Michelle's parents and family. Michelle and Audrea were as close as best friends could be. As I stood by her casket greeting more family and friends, I took great comfort that Michelle would live again, that eternally nothing had happened to her, and that she was safe, filled with joy, and engaged in a new work.

Before the funeral services began, I knelt down and offered a family prayer. I prayed for peace, for healing in the lives of Michael and Sam and in the lives of the family and friends gathered there. I expressed my gratitude for Jesus Christ, for the faith I had in Him, and for the hope we could have for a better world, "even at the right hand of God." I arose and proceeded to close the caskets one by one. I began with Anna. She had not sustained any external physical injury and looked as if she were just asleep. And then I closed the casket of Benjamin. I don't know how I could have endured that process without a firm witness that it would be only temporary and that they would rise again.

I then came to the casket of my wife. After the accident I had been told that the young child she was carrying was developed enough for him to be taken from the womb and prepared to be buried with Michelle. The young boy we were going to name William was dressed in a white baby blessing gown and lovingly nestled in the arms of my wife. It was the first time I had seen him, and I was overcome with how much he resembled Samuel when he was born. Perhaps there was no greater, honorable way for such a mother in Israel to be buried than that, knowing that

Michael between two of the caskets

in the resurrection she would rise with a child in her arms, ready to carry on the boundless work of being a mother.

We entered the chapel and listened to a beautiful service of praise and honor in their behalf, and then escorted their bodies to their final resting place. It was a very sweet experience to again feel the support and love of my family, friends, and the community throughout the day. At the graveside, I again offered a prayer that those who were gathered would feel the peace that was sustaining my family and that they could be comforted with the understanding that "all is well."

After the prayer, as we remained at the graveside talking with those who had come, I had the opportunity to meet the parents of Cameron White. We embraced each other as companions on this new, difficult journey together. Can you imagine the misery that could have been heaped upon them in their darkest hour of grief had I chosen not to take the Lord's path of forgiveness? That sweet, blessed day could have been eternally marred by bitterness, anger, resentment, and maybe even hatred, had I not allowed the

Savior to take the burden and exercised faith in Him. I felt so very blessed that I had been spared that trial.

My family and I stayed at the graveside, thanking those who had come to pay their respects, as we looked at the three coffins ready to be lowered into their final resting places. The flowers adorning the caskets were beautiful, the snow-capped mountains framed against a blue sky were picturesque, and the peace and joy that we felt was reassuring and sustaining.

We returned to the stake center, which was the church building where the funeral had been held, and then drove to the meetinghouse where I served as a bishop. Many of the women in our congregation had prepared a wonderful meal for us to enjoy as a family. It was such a treat to talk with them in that setting and dine on the food they had provided. I felt as if I was eating my first real meal since the crash.

Later that evening I pondered what that meeting at the graveside between Ron and Marilyn White and I might have looked like, how it must have been pleasing to heaven to see such love.

I knew that the adversary works tirelessly to steal our peace and turn us against each other. *We all make mistakes, sometimes with terrible consequences,* I reminded myself. We say something that should never have been said, we do something that should never have been done, we misunderstand, misrepresent, or misinterpret, and our actions or words create hurt in our own lives and in the lives of others. And there are those who suffer cruelties at the hands of others. I thought of the five people whose lives ended Monday night at Trolley Square. And yet He who knows that these and so many other kinds of tragedies would occur commanded us to combat them with love. He knows that when we're hurt, we're vulnerable and thus susceptible to grudges, hidden wedges, and wounds, all of which, if left unchecked, could fester into anger, retribution, vilification, even hatred.

Without the necessary healing the Savior provides, over time we may begin to wonder why we're not as happy as we used to be, why we're a little more critical, a little less patient, and more judgmental, why we withhold our love and affection rather than give it—all the while feeling more miserable, rather than joyful in this life.

I recalled in my mind the many experiences of the last week preceding the viewing and the funeral and the roller coaster of emotions propelling me from the extreme highs of peace to the depths of sadness and grief, over and over. What an opportunity for the adversary to kick me when I was down, to finish me off and heap added misery into my life had I chosen to not follow the Savior's command and "let it go." How seemingly easy and justifiable it would have been for me to join him in his misery, to get angry, to vilify, to lash out at this life and how wrong everything in it had just become. I recalled the darkness I felt before my wife reminded me to "buck up!"

The Savior had suffered all so that we would not have to. He said He would take our burdens, and He repeated the invitation to give them to Him while He ministered in the flesh, and He has since reminded us what He accomplished in the Atonement. There's no way I was or ever will be strong enough to bear *that* burden I was presented on the night of the crash. It was immediately given to the Lord at His command, and I instead took upon me His light burden and easy yoke of serving and loving others—having full faith in the Savior and in His ability to bear my heavy burden and to heal my family.

• • •

14

"Get Busy Serving Others"

On Sunday Michael and I attended the church meeting held at the chapel within the hospital. It was a wonderful service, and the spirit was quite strong; however, as I sat in that hospital chapel, my thoughts were with my home congregation, desiring to feel of their love and support as I had the prior Sunday. During the day, we noticed that Sam had begun to improve quite rapidly. He was much more active and aware, not quite as somber as he had been. He was progressing in his physical rehabilitation and starting to solve, with increased ease, the puzzles and games used to test his progress. We began to consult with the nurses about when he might be able to go home, and we took hope that perhaps he could be released within the week if he continued to improve.

On Monday morning his condition had improved sufficiently from the previous day, and we were discussing the possibility of leaving the hospital, perhaps within three or four days.

By the next morning, Tuesday, February 20, Sam was well

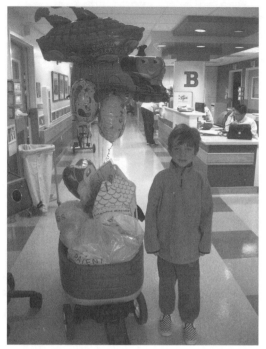

Sam leaving the hospital, February 20, 2007, to go home

enough to come home. I could see the hand of the Savior healing him miraculously in His own way and time. I think it was enough for Sam to have viewed the body of our neighbor Dewey and to have heard his mother telling him that even though all die, we will all live again. He was mercifully spared having to attend the funeral of his mother, sister, and brother—a possibly traumatizing event for a six-year-old.

We gathered up all of the letters, pictures, posters, stuffed animals, books, and other expressions of encouragement and hope that had been sent for Sam, carefully placed him in the car, and then I drove Sam and Michael home. As we pulled up to our home, we were again appreciative of the ribbons that adorned the trees around our house. Inside the home there were more notes, flowers, and balloons that had previously been tied to the trees and shrubs around our home. Sam slowly walked into my room and slipped into my bed. I said goodnight to the family members who had accompanied us to our home, and then I went downstairs to pray with Michael before he went to sleep.

When I came back upstairs, I was surprised to see that Sam was still awake. As I proceeded to adjust the sheets and pillows, I saw that his eyes were fixed on mine, and he was looking at me with a confused expression on his face. Given his unflinching stare, I thought he might need something, so I looked into his eyes without saying anything, trying not to cry before I found out what he needed. He then asked, "Where's Mom?"

Tears welled in my eyes, and I dropped to my knees by his side. I hid my face in my hands and quickly pleaded for heavenly help in telling him what had happened. I looked up and said that there had been a terrible crash, and that his mother and Ben and Anna were dead. He looked down at the sheets, and then away into the distance, showing no emotion. I placed my face in my hands and begged that Michelle would be there for her son. I suddenly felt as if I couldn't take it anymore; I was so desperately alone without my wife. Sam never again asked where his mother was, but in the days and weeks that followed, he frequently cried out for her to be there with him.

I turned out the lights and crawled into the bed. I was a single father to two boys living in a house that was growing quieter as the echoes of activity and commotion that had once filled that home faded further and further away. I had been told while in the hospital that I was entering my "year of firsts," but I didn't quite appreciate what that meant until, as we settled into our new circumstances, I realized we were just a few days from what would have been Ben's twelfth birthday on February 25.

We started preparations to celebrate the day, but it was so very difficult to have an upbeat celebration of his life when he had so recently left us. We gathered family and some friends together and tried our best, but it was in many ways a very empty day and underscored the larger-than-life presence he had been in our home. The twenty-fifth of February was no longer a day to celebrate my wonderful son's birthday, it was the first birthday party for Ben that we would celebrate since his passing. Welcome to the "year of firsts."

The next week I made arrangements for someone to watch over Sam so I could attend and serve in the Salt Lake Temple. *Perhaps I'll finally be able to feel Michelle's presence*, I thought. As I participated in the worship services, I never felt any special significant indication that she was there. There was a sweet, peaceful spirit present, but nothing particular to Michelle, or Ben and Anna. As I sat in one of the interior rooms, almost trying to force some kind of special reconnection with my family, I did finally feel something. It wasn't Michelle, or the children, but it was the Spirit conveying the same message from them, particularly from Michelle, that I had already received many times before: "They are busy." In fact, the words "we're busy" specifically came into my mind. I knew that; I had received that answer many times before, but I wanted to know "doing what?" As I sat pondering that question, I felt that they were aware of everything that we were passing through and were mindful of us. I sensed they were petitioning our Father in Heaven on our behalf, but Michelle was letting me know in no uncertain terms that she had an immense amount of work to do on the other side, and she couldn't be in two places at once. There was another new instruction that then came into my mind as I thought, *I need to get busy too*. I could almost hear Michelle telling me to "get busy serving others." I had invited others to extend acts of service, and I needed to do the same.

* * *

The first Mother's Day without Michelle was a particularly difficult day for me to deal with, struggling as I was to move forward in life without my best friend. Prompted by what I had felt while worshiping in the temple, and surely with some inspiration from Michelle, I found my heart aching for Marilyn, Cameron's mother, and the trial she too was passing through. I wrapped up a Mother's Day present, wrote a note of encouragement, and took it to her house with Sam and Michael. No one was home, so I left the book and card on their doorstep. (I later found out that they had gone as a family to place flowers on Michelle's grave.) I returned to my car and looked back at their house. I felt such a love and empathy for her as I stood in front of the darkened house. I'll never forget how it impacted me for good. It helped heal my pain, knowing that the Savior too was looking at their family with a love so much more powerful than what I felt. Michelle was right; there is strength and healing in service.

A few days after Mother's Day, during my early morning gospel study, I read a talk suggesting that starting a day with a prayer to be led to someone who needed help was a prayer that was always answered by the Lord. Prompted to do so, I knelt at the table and offered such a prayer, and then went about my daily routine, thinking nothing more of it. On the way back to my home office after lunch, I pulled into a gas station, and another car pulled in immediately behind me. It was Ron, Cameron's father. We talked as brothers, moving through this difficult circumstance united in love for one another. I cannot help but think that our meeting that day was a direct answer to the prayer I offered that morning, blessing both of us with healing, peace, and love.

Soon after, I started to experience what I had expressed right after the tragedy, that "heaven would not be heaven without Cameron being with his family." I began to feel of the desire our Savior has for each of His children, individually and by name, to return home to Him without losing anyone.

In those first few weeks after the crash, as I pressed forward in my life, I had thought that I had learned what I needed to learn from the experience. I focused on healing as I tried to move forward, tending to my boys and their progress while hoping that my emotional swings would begin to temper. The grieving was at times very intense, triggering a regular release of all sorts of chemicals into my bloodstream, as if I was on a new type of naturally occurring morphine pump, only I had yet to figure out how to control the amount. I knew with a surety that Michelle, Ben, and Anna were happy and busy serving others. I knew and felt they wanted me to be happy too by getting busy and serving others, but I was still allowed to be exposed to intense emotional contradictions that were teaching me additional lessons about the work of our Father in Heaven and how to minister with authenticity in that work. I had no idea that those lessons and experiences would be utilized so soon and in such a public forum.

• • •

15

The Box

Cameron was just three months shy of his eighteenth birthday on the evening of the crash, three months from becoming an "adult," according to the legally recognized definition. Had he already turned eighteen, there would be no question as to where his trial would occur, but because he had not yet crossed that threshold, the initial legal proceedings were focused not on his guilt or innocence, but whether he should be prosecuted in the juvenile or the adult court. There were significant ramifications to the final decision. If he were certified to stand trial as an adult, he could receive a prison sentence of up to twenty-five years due to the number of fatalities caused by the crash. If he stood trial as a juvenile, he would be held in a juvenile corrective system only until he turned twenty-one, and then he would be released regardless of the progress he had made.

The certification hearing was held at the main court complex in downtown Salt Lake City on June 4, 2007. Reporters and cameras were once again present to capture statements and reactions from my family and from Cameron's attorneys. The district attorney's office wanted to see Cameron tried as an adult, arguing that he was old enough to be held fully accountable for his decisions and actions that night and that three month's difference in age should not disqualify him from that outcome.

Cameron, wearing an orange jumpsuit, slowly entered the courtroom and sat at the defendant's table. It was the first time I had seen him in person. The proceedings began and, amidst the initial legal motions, he and I shared a quiet, personal moment when our eyes met and he mouthed the words "I'm sorry" to me. I managed a half-smile to my face as I nodded to him in acknowledgment. I had wondered what emotions I would feel when I first saw him and how I would react. I once again felt the Savior's love for him and his family, the same that I had felt when I had looked on their house on Mother's Day.

The proceedings were exquisitely difficult to sit through. The district attorney's office began the certification hearing by first establishing the horrific nature of the crash, including specific details of how violent the impact had been, complete with pictures of my wife and children that were shown to the judge. The judge had issued an initial plea to the prosecutors that he not be shown the pictures as those images are difficult to forget. I did not have to see them, but just knowing that those pictures existed was very unsettling to me because my imagination began to fill in the blanks based upon what I had seen that night.

I had met with a victim's advocate court representative prior to the hearing and was told that at some point during the proceedings I could be called to the stand. Given what I was experiencing as I sat in the courtroom with my two sons and the rest of my family, and the evidence and information that was being presented, I had some concerns about myself. Would I be tempted to let my emotions overpower the commitment I had made to let it go? Would I be tempted to entertain thoughts about the judicial process itself, passing judgment on what I thought was transpiring, without the background or experience to objectively understand? Would I think that mercy was robbing justice and they were going too easy on him, or that justice wasn't considering mercy and they were being too harsh? How could I be completely confident in, and satisfied with, the outcome?

Midway through the proceedings, the district attorney's representative called me to the stand to further establish the devastating effect Cameron's choices had on my family that night. I have since tried to recall what I said on the stand. I can only distinctly remember the answer I gave when the judge asked what sentence I thought was appropriate for Cameron. I told him that on February 9, 2007, both Cameron and I had "already been handed a life sentence," and that I now wanted "what was best for Cameron." I explained that I did not want to take any culpability whatsoever for the final decision, and I answered his question by saying that I believed it was solely the judge's responsibility to settle questions determining the final consequence, and I would fully support whatever decision he made. The *Deseret News* reported that I additionally encouraged Cameron to honor the memory of those who died by "making something of his life."

I felt so liberated the moment after answering the judge's question because I realized I would never have to carry the massive weight of the establishment of the consequence. What if the decision or punishment I thought he should receive was different than the one announced by the judge, who was the only one in authority to actually make that decision? I'm thankful that I didn't try to take that responsibility away from the judge and place it upon myself. I am grateful for a judicial system that, although imperfect, dealt with this weighty matter and freed me from yet another burden I could have been tempted to think I could carry. I am also especially thankful for the victim's advocate group that protected and assisted my family throughout the process.

The judge certified Cameron to stand trial as a juvenile, and he turned him over to the juvenile courts' custodial care. After the decision was announced, a few members of my family and I were again invited to address Cameron. I don't recall what I said, but the *Deseret News* reported that I encouraged Cameron to "make use of the 'wonderful resources' available for rehabilitation and hoped that [he] would always remember the heartbreaking night as a turning point in his life, one that would commit him to 'become a productive member of society.'" It was also reported that I "hoped this would be an example to the community as well and that people would 'seek for peace and healing rather than looking for retribution' in tragic cases" (Linda Thompson, "Young DUI driver to 'secure facility,'" *Deseret News,* June 5, 2007).

We arose as the judge left the room. As I watched Cameron escorted from the courtroom, shuffling slowly through the door, I became aware of a mental process I had subconsciously been using with every thought that involved him since the night of the crash. When Cameron passed through the doorway into the next room and the door was closed behind him, in my mind he went "back into the box," and it too was closed.

To keep my commitment to myself, I had had to isolate Cameron as an individual in my mind. When it was necessary to consider him or his family at the graveside, on Mother's Day, or here in the court, I could open that box and go through those situations with heavenly assistance, but after those moments passed, all that was associated specifically with Cameron, the individual, went back into the box in my mind, and it was again shut. I was able to move through my healing process without Cameron being a part of that process or becoming a target of the more powerful emotions I experienced. In the midst of each grief- or pain-filled moment I endured, accompanied by a spectrum of emotions, my pleas for healing and relief were directed toward the Savior rather than at the "person who had caused this to happen" in my life.

It was a blessing that I was given this empowering way of enduring the mourning, frustration, grieving, loving, crying, laughing, and gratitude that I was experiencing by mentally controlling who participated in those memories, thoughts, and feelings. In exchange for giving the burden to the Lord, I was given full control over my life, including who would and would not be a conscious part of it. If I were tempted to give up that mental control by allowing thoughts of helplessness or victimization, I had only to reflect on that moment in the car, that terrible moment in February when I truly did not have control over who was, or was not, a part of my life.

Perhaps the protection that the mental box afforded was no more pronounced than when, in my weakness, I felt the emotion of anger. The adversary is ruthless in beating you violently when you are down. I was frequently tempted to join the adversary in his misery, by opening the box and directing those powerful emotions on the person whose decision had caused me to be in this situation, potentially fueling my pride and self-justification in so doing.

My commitment to "let it go" was a commitment to exercise my faith and direct my weaknesses toward the Savior for strength, and He in return repeatedly empowered me to keep that box tightly shut. In prayer with my Heavenly Father, I would vent my frustrations and anger, "wrestling with the Lord" as it were, and then I would be greatly humbled as I was reminded of my Savior, Jesus Christ. Then I could ponder His life, His example, His patience and long-suffering and finally feel a greater strength to stay true to the commitment I had made and move forward. It was wonderfully difficult schooling in how to go from just enduring something, to enduring it well by controlling the only thing I could really control, my will.

• • •

Later that evening, after the court proceedings were finished, I wondered how I had created this coping device I called "the box." I recalled an experience I had after returning from my missionary service that had prepared me to mentally separate and isolate things as a way to process or work through them.

I wanted a car to get to school and work, and my father wisely counseled me to think utilitarian and inexpensive. As we looked for an economy car, I increasingly began to consider what that car would say about me as a person. There was, after all, a nicer, "cooler" car that I was drawn to, not much more money than the car my father recommended. To save on the cost, I trimmed off every option I could, including air conditioning. Since I live in what is often referred to as a cultivated desert, it gets very hot in the summer. I guess my idea of being "cool" included beads of sweat running down my face during the summer. In hindsight, if I could beam myself back in time and confront myself, I wouldn't say anything to the young me, I would just walk up and slug myself in the gut for being so stupid, and then whisper in my Dad's ear, "Buy Apple stock!"

I worked at a music store in a mall selling pianos and

grandfather clocks. Between car payments, I was able to save enough to buy the next object of my desire, a very nice stereo system for the car. One night after work, I emerged from the mall and made the long trek to my car. As I opened the door, the center console light illuminated a scene of horror and devastation. My stereo was gone, replaced by a large gaping hole surrounded by a disfigured dash. The anger came instantly. *Who would do this!* I thought. I ran back to the mall, frantically searching for the closest pay phone (no cell phones then). I dialed 911 and practically screamed at the operator that I was a victim of a terrible crime! "Someone has broken into my car and stolen my car stereo!" I exclaimed. I meticulously described exactly what I had found and where the car was located. I was assured that a patrol car would be sent over to investigate.

I raced back to the car fully expecting to hear a siren in the distance making its way toward my vehicle. I waited and waited, listening intently for the siren, looking left and right to ensure the policeman located me. *Perhaps they'll catch the thief,* I thought, anticipating a quick response. I began pacing outside the car. Fifteen minutes, then twenty minutes passed. *Where are they?* I thought. Thirty minutes had elapsed; the thief was surely uncatchable by that time. I looked upward at the stars and began a prayer of desperation. He knew what I was going through, and surely He could help bring about some swift justice. As soon as I started to pray, I felt a very different sensation come over me—a sense of embarrassment and shame as I felt suddenly exposed. I had allowed myself to be duped by the things of the world.

A picture began forming in my mind. I saw two individuals standing side by side. Under the person on the right, I saw a list start to form as if it were being typed, line after line. It read in part, "Loving family, Gospel blessings, supportive friends, educational opportunities, good health, a job." The list developed rapidly and continued to grow and grow. Under the person on the left, the list was compiled much more slowly: "no family support, poor friends, no love, limited opportunities." My analysis of the second list was interrupted when the face of the person on the right became recognizable. It was my own. The person on the left remained a faceless figure, and I knew that it represented the person who had taken my stereo. The picture disappeared, and my chastening began. My anger dissipated as well.

More than forty minutes had passed when the squad car finally approached me, without lights or siren sounding. I'm sure it was a busy night for the police, and they had correctly prioritized their calls. By then, I didn't even want to report the theft. The picture I had had in my mind helped me separate and process how I could react to those situations in the future. I didn't have to wait for the thief to be caught; I could immediately mentally arrest him and place him in a "lock box" in my mind. I would then be left with complete control over how I reacted to the loss, while regaining the peace in my life that was interrupted.

To help me keep that commitment and remember what I had learned that night, I decided not to fix the dash of my car. My conviction was certainly tested as that stupid, wonderful car was broken into three more times. But learning to control how I reacted to the offenses of others was a critical lesson to learn, and the image in my mind helped me understand that I should never judge another, especially when I thought I was right. Driving that car with a ruined dash for another nine years was a great way to continually remind myself of what I learned that night.

• • •

16

What Have You Lost?

I was shocked how increasingly lonely it was living without
Michelle, Ben, and Anna in our home and how physically painful
loneliness is. I was surprised how I could be in my house, surrounded by loved ones, or be out among friends and still feel so
incredibly alone.

In my experience, the mornings were the worst. Waking at
three or four o'clock in the morning ready to cry isn't a great way
to start the day. The emotional roller coaster wasn't much fun
either, and I didn't want to stay on it. Instead of being advised to
"keep your hands inside the vehicle at all times and have fun" on
this particular ride, the best warning would be "you're strapped
in until the ride comes to a complete stop, so don't fight it."

I also found that it was possible to become too sad. In those
situations, my emotions stopped helping me heal and would instead pull me downward into a free fall. On one particular night
in the middle of June, I not only found myself spiraling downward, propelled by the loneliness, but I felt as if there was no

one to turn to or call at that late hour for help. I prayed, but I still struggled to have faith. I was beset by an enormous attack of self-pity, and I felt that no one could comprehend my terrible situation; I didn't know anyone else who had lost a spouse and children so suddenly. My mind once again revisited the scene of the crash. I was letting it all come back, and it was crushing my hopes and progress in the process.

I cried for so long it hurt. My body sunk to the floor, and the image of a plane headed for a fiery crash came into my mind. I've never flown a plane, but I have played flight simulator games on the computer that mimic what it would be like in the cockpit. Whenever I would put the simulated plane into a nosedive, the warning system would audibly give the command to "Pull up! Pull up! Pull up!" I heard that warning in a pronounced way in my mind as I lay on the floor, so I stood up and left the house for a long walk. After a few hours of pondering and praying as I walked, I slowly felt the comfort I sought; I had avoided a horrific emotional crash. For me, that command to "pull up" became a very helpful phrase to repeat when I felt I was passing through too much and couldn't take it anymore. With some practice, I got to the point that whenever I felt myself getting too sad, I would hear in my mind the rehearsed, repeated command to "Pull up! Pull up! Pull up!"

I know that the adversary wants to make us miserable; he wants us to be as miserable as he is, to put our thoughts in those moments of turbulent sadness into a tailspin of hopelessness and injustice. Mercifully, after that experience, whenever the adversary would try to disrupt my journey forward, I would respond literally to "pull up" by tilting my face heavenward—no matter where I was—and I then found I was once again ascending on my journey toward my Father in Heaven. However, like any

Anna dancing

adversary, Satan persistently looked for other ways to disrupt my healing and growing peace as time passed.

One evening I was tempted to start listing all the things I had lost. I thought of the summer and fall trips we used to take as a family that we would no longer take; Anna's dance recitals that I was no longer attending; the scouting activities I wouldn't be able to have with Ben; and many other disruptions that had come into our family. I thought of Michelle, wishing she were still by my side sharing our lives together, and realized that I would not be able to experience more of my life with her. As I started to go into a mental tailspin, the practiced alarm sounded in my mind to "pull up," only that time I really struggled to change the course of my emotions. The phrase "I can't believe everything I've lost" kept passing through my mind, over and over, with each new part of my life that I realized had changed forever or that I would never get to experience. That unhelpful phrase was drowning out the command to "pull up," and I was headed for a mental disaster.

In my growing despair, I began to pray earnestly. I had barely started to plead for help when I felt the Spirit so strongly, and a question formed in my mind that stopped my plunge: "What have you lost?" I knew it was meant more as a mild rebuke than as an actual query for me to respond to. I was initially surprised by the question, so simple and straightforward, yet powerful and full of profound meaning.

In just four words my mind was spiritually grabbed and turned to focus on the eternal plan of salvation and happiness, remembering that with an eternal perspective and an ability to see things as they really are, I had not lost anything; all "losses" would be made up to me through Jesus Christ. The Holy Spirit had just done what Michelle had often done to help me focus on the truth. If she were telling me something important, and she felt I wasn't giving her instruction enough attention, she would reach up and grab my jaw and turn my face so it was facing hers and I could look her directly in the eyes. It was always effective, but not often pleasant. That time my view had been quickly turned upward to heaven.

As I pondered that question in response to my tally of what I had lost, I was further reminded that if I remained faithful and didn't give up, I could gain everything that Heavenly Father had. But I needed to "buck up," "pull up," keep the commandments, and get busy serving others. It was an invitation to keep going forward until, with the passage of time, I could look at my situation from the perspective of my Father in Heaven. To really appreciate the blessings I was being given and the limitless blessings that awaited me if I stayed faithful, I had to look at them from the eternal vantage point of the Giver.

The day after that incident, a group of friends came by my home to pay a visit. I recounted the details of what I had experienced the evening of the crash, adding that the road where the crash occurred had been very busy that night because a high school basketball game had just ended, and there were many cars passing through that underpass along with my family's car. I recounted some of the experiences I had had since the crash, relating to my perspective of that tragedy, and said that "of all the families on the road that night, my family was the best prepared to be hit." I couldn't believe what I had just said, yet I pronounced it as an absolute truth, and I still believe it is. Later that evening as I prayed, I again recalled the many experiences that had prepared our family for that evening. It was yet another way of saying "Why not me?" when I had been tempted to think *Why me?*

• • •

17

To Minister with Authenticity

Toward the end of July, the impression that I needed to serve others intensified. I knew it was the best antidote for grieving, but I didn't exactly know how I could help others because of what I had gone through. I was still serving as the bishop to my congregation, and serving my family raising my two sons, but I hadn't been able yet to connect how the tragedy would specifically bless the lives of others through my service.

The first week of July, Michael, Sam, and I, along with Michelle's family, decided to go to San Diego for our annual vacation. It was a trip that Michelle and I, with our children, had made every year since we were married. Although we knew it would be a very difficult trip to make as a family of three, especially considering the many memories associated with that area, we still decided to go and spend some time at the beach together. We didn't go looking for closure, we were just ready to get away for a while and be together. We stayed in the same condominium that we always used in San Diego, and we went to the same beach and the same restaurants. In every way we tried to make the trip as normal an experience as we possibly could, even though it was anything but the same.

Early in the week, as I was walking through the condominium hallway, I met a woman and her daughter who were also from Utah. The woman said I looked familiar and asked if I was the man who had lost half of his family in a car crash in February. I said I was, and she expressed her sorrow for that tragedy. She further explained that she lived very close to the crash site and travelled the freeway underpass frequently. Perhaps it was her way of saying, "That could have been me in the crash that night." She and her husband had come on this trip with all their grown children and spouses and all of their grandchildren too.

Throughout the week as we would subsequently pass each other in the condo halls, we were no longer strangers but new-found neighbors, exchanging brief updates on how our vacations were going. Toward the end of our stay, I saw one of the grown daughters exit the elevator with her children. As I approached to say hello, I could see that she was visibly upset. I asked if everything was all right. She began to cry and said, "My father passed away yesterday." Their whole family had gone to Anaheim, and while her father was visiting friends who lived there, he suffered a heart attack.

I desperately wanted to be of some assistance, but she was busy assisting her mother and siblings, arranging for the transportation of her father's body back to Salt Lake City. Through tear-filled eyes I could only think to say, "I will keep you in my prayers." As we parted I thought, *Surely there is something more I can do,* but I didn't know what it was.

The next day Sam, Michael, and I were relaxing on the beach when I noticed their entire family huddled together in a circle a few hundred feet from where we were. I saw the woman I had met at the beginning of our vacation surrounded by her children and their spouses, and all of the grandchildren. I watched as the grandchildren wrote notes in the sand, surely expressions of love for their grandfather.

As I looked on this tender scene, I was moved to tears. I again wanted to help that new widow in any way that I could, feeling that I could relate somewhat to what she might be going through, so suddenly losing her husband, companion, and best friend of so many years. I could comprehend her grief better than I ever would have been able to before the crash. I earnestly prayed for help and direction in my desire to say something that would help bring her additional peace. As I prayed, nothing specific came to my mind, every sentence I constructed sounded trite and cliché. *What can I possibly say?* I thought, still searching for words of comfort that I could offer. I suddenly felt a specific prompting to just get up and walk toward them. I immediately rose from my chair and made my way down the beach to where she stood, still surrounded by her children and grandchildren.

As I walked into the circle and toward the widow, I didn't say anything, and they, knowing who I was, didn't say anything to me. I approached her, and she began to come toward me. We simply embraced each other. There was nothing that needed to be said; I think she needed to feel that there was someone else with her on this new path she was now travelling, that there was some-one else in this world at that moment who could comprehend what she was feeling. I know the comfort she felt was the Savior's; I was just a vessel for that message of love, understanding, and encouragement from the source of all peace.

I know that Jesus Christ, having passed through everything, can fully relate to anything that we might experience here on earth, but on this particular day and for that specific widow, He wasn't able to be there physically in person, but He was able to be there through the Holy Spirit and through one who was willing to stand in His stead. I felt very blessed to be able to be that person through whom He could extend His love, His grace, His message of peace to that woman.

Later that evening as I pondered that sacred healing moment in both of our lives, the Spirit reinforced something that I had studied many times from the life of a much-loved leader in the Church named Neal A. Maxwell, who was diagnosed with leukemia in 1996. In March of 2000, while he was pondering why he had been afflicted by this illness, Elder Maxwell felt the Spirit whisper that "I have given you leukemia that you might teach my people with authenticity" (Bruce C. Hafen, *A Disciple's Life: The Biography of Neal A. Maxwell* [Salt Lake City: Deseret Book, 2002], 562).

The trials that I had been allowed to pass through were preparing me, in a very small way, to be a better minister to those who were experiencing similar trials and tests. To be effective, it had to come from my heart. I again recalled what I had learned about having a broken heart—one that had been broken in the same way that one would break a horse, so it no longer ran wild and independent, but was willing to submit to the tug of the reins and go in the direction needed. I had to learn to minister with a heart that is contrite, humble, teachable—one that trials and suffering tend to engender. That day, in an infinitely small way, I gained a greater appreciation for the Atonement of Jesus Christ; that by virtue of what He passed through, He could minister with complete and perfect authenticity to a widow standing so newly alone on the beach, surrounded by her family.

Our vacation to San Diego was not very easy for me to enjoy.

I struggled throughout the trip, recalling so many sweet memories of Michelle, Ben, and Anna. It was harder to sleep there than it was at our house, and I would wander in the early morning hours from our condo down to the beach to walk and ponder. I was amazed at how many people were up at all hours of the night and early morning, hanging out on the boardwalk or at the beach. In hindsight, it probably wasn't the safest place to be.

Michelle had always enjoyed roaming the beach early in the morning looking for seashells as the tide receded back into the ocean. When I would accompany her on these beach strolls, I would often be distracted by the beach detritus: the seaweed with the flies that would take to the air in unison as we approached a freshly washed-up pile, or the garbage that was left by slovenly beachgoers or that had just washed in from the sea. I thought it was a wonderful way to spend time talking with Michelle, but I wasn't terribly interested in finding shells. She, on the other hand, was much wiser than I as she combed the beach, intently looking for treasures. She had a wonderful ability to focus beyond the dross and distraction when looking for seashells, and she was a very patient seeker—throwing back those that didn't make the cut and looking instead for the keepers. Those shells she would wash off and take with her back to our home in Salt Lake, carefully preserving and saving them to enjoy again and again. After nineteen years of making that yearly trek to San Diego, she had amassed quite a collection of seashells. To my eye, it was just a large jar full of common seashells and nothing more. For her, it was a collection of priceless, captured moments.

As I walked the beach in the early morning hours on this first trip without Michelle, I didn't focus on the smell, the flies, the sand, or the garbage. Instead I looked for Michelle searching for those seashells. I could see that, for my wife, those shells were a tangible symbol of her happiness in the moment she found them. And when they were washed off and preserved, they provided help for her in the days when she wanted to recall a happy memory. They had always been prominently displayed in the front room of our home where she could look on them and recall the moment, refocus her joy, and move forward with renewed energy and purpose.

Since the crash, I have mentally combed my life for those treasures, anxiously searching for my "seashells" in life. That became a wonderful mental exercise to focus on when I sometimes wanted to give up. As any beachcomber knows, those treasures don't stay exposed forever; you have to seize the moment to capture them before they're washed back out to sea or covered in time by sand. The many wonderful memories that I had, of San Diego or of any place we had been, became part of a new collection, placed prominently in my mind so that I could recall them quickly when I began to struggle to move forward.

The many opportunities to serve others have also become part of my growing collection of seashells. They allow me to see things with a new perspective, to recall the happiness, and to enjoy overwhelming gratitude that I had those experiences at all. Those seashells in life are as tangible to me as the seashells found on the beach.

• • •

18

The Latter More Blessed
Than the Beginning

Working from home had always been an immeasurable blessing in my life; I wouldn't trade the time spent close to my children for anything. That summer, with my two sons spending
much of their vacation at their friends' homes rather than in their
very empty house, I was often left alone at home wishing I had
somewhere to go for work.

Unwilling to let the weekly yard and house maintenance suffice, I embarked on a significant remodel of the house, working
from the list of home-improvement projects Michelle and I had
wanted to pursue.

I decided to move my office from the basement into the room
that Anna and Sam had shared upstairs, while moving Sam closer
to Michael who was downstairs. I couldn't bear to keep Ben and
Anna's rooms as some type of untouched shrine to the way things
once had been, so I began the heartbreaking process of putting
their belongings into storage. I soon found that it wasn't going to
be a quick process. It was a multi-week struggle just to clean out

their rooms; each piece of clothing or collected trinket was tied to so many memories and became so difficult to entomb in a plastic storage bin.

As I was completing that horrible task, I temporarily moved my office to the kitchen table before relocating it to Anna's room. "Going to work" became a process of setting up my laptop and spreading various papers and files across the kitchen table. As the days progressed, the notes, memos, bills, and other mail spilled onto the chairs and finally onto the floor. Much of the paperwork spread about the room was generated by the many medical and funeral expenses and the accompanying insurance correspondence.

◆ ◆ ◆

In the shock and emotionally charged weeks immediately after the crash, I hadn't wanted to deal with any financial issues. While picking caskets and vaults and multiplying all the costs by three, I jokingly asked the representative from the mortuary what would happen if, after the funeral, I didn't pay. "How would you get your caskets back?" I asked. I don't think he really appreciated my black humor in that situation, although Michelle's brothers who were with me enjoyed a lighthearted moment in the midst of that most heart-wrenching task.

When Sam and I were in the hospital, I likewise didn't consider the costs of the treatment, thinking that the health insurance would take care of most of the charges. *That is why I have health insurance in the first place*, I thought. Yet sitting at the kitchen table, working through the health care bills and ensuring each charge was paid felt like a full-time job.

One evening as I left Michael in charge of Sam and began

a lengthy walk-and-ponder session through my neighborhood, I wondered if the insurance would be adequate to cover all of the costs. As I mentally tallied the bills, I felt impressed to focus my mind on a different kind of total when I asked myself these questions: *What is the financial value of a faithful example? What price would I put on my commitment to "let it go," forgive, and exercise faith in the healing ability of Jesus Christ?*

I thought of Michael and Sam and of the eternal value they would receive from the example set by their father. The list of priceless blessings grew as I progressed on my walk through the neighborhood. I felt I needed to focus my energy on healing my family, trusting that the Lord would enable me to provide for them as a single parent, as well as take care of the medical and funeral expenses. My desire to exercise faith in my Savior was followed with a test of that faith.

One of the letters that arrived after most of the bills had been covered was a notification that all of Sam's hospital expenses initially paid for by my employer's health insurance program were going to be subject to subrogation. That's a legal way of saying that buried deep in the terms of my health insurance policy was a statement that said my company could recoup expenses for a claim it paid out if another insurance company paid a settlement related to the expense. They now wanted my auto insurance to cover the more than $50,000 the health insurance had already paid out.

I was further notified that my ambulance ride and one night luxury stay at the local ICU, which had initially been covered, should not have been covered because I had been taken to an out-of-network provider without getting prior approval. *Perhaps I should have called them before I let the emergency crews take me from the car*, I thought sarcastically.

I was assured that there was a process to take care of all of these technicalities, but after several weeks of making phone calls, sending letters, getting clarifications and documentation, only to receive payment denials and additional bills, it seemed the only way I would get out of this situation was to just pay all of the expenses out of pocket. As I prayerfully considered my situation, I was reminded to have faith. Fortunately my faith in financial matters had been strengthened and refined because of an experience I had had six years earlier.

• • •

In March 2001, I was abruptly laid off from a struggling technology firm. Within a few weeks, I had a job offer at an Internet startup company with impressive prospects. But when I prayed about the opportunity and discussed it with Michelle, I felt that I should not accept the offer, so I turned it down. My thoughts turned instead to a company that I had previously worked for called Informix Software, so I contacted some of my former colleagues there to see if there were any job opportunities available.

I was surprised to learn there was a job opening in the territory. They were excited to bring me back on board if I was interested. I turned in my job application, quite hopeful to start within a few weeks. Two days later it was announced that Informix would be acquired by IBM. I called my friends at Informix and was told there was an immediate freeze on all new hiring. The image of a bird in the hand and two in the bush came into my head, and I wondered if I had done the right thing in turning down the offer I had received earlier. As I prayed about this new twist of events, I was assured that everything would work out and that I would indeed be hired by Informix; I just needed to have patience and faith.

For the next three months I remained in regular contact with the hiring manager at Informix and was continually assured that he was trying to "push things through." But just as we were leaving for our yearly vacation to San Diego, he called me and said, "We've tried everything possible to get your name approved to hire, and unfortunately they have just cancelled all the open requisitions." There wasn't going to be a job offer from Informix Software.

My hopes were crushed, and I wondered how I had received that inspiration and peace; *I felt that answer regarding Informix so distinctly,* I thought. In a quiet moment during our family trip, I knelt and pleaded with the Lord for direction and help. Once again I was specifically impressed by the Holy Spirit that I would be hired by Informix Software, and I was additionally chastened for my lack of faith in the initial answer. I needed to "cast not away therefore [my] confidence" in the answer I had received, and I was in "need of patience" in the test I was enduring (Hebrews 10:35–36).

Perhaps the greatest blessing I received during this extended time off from work was deciding to run my first marathon. I bought a pair of running shoes and set out on a training plan for an October race in St. George, Utah. The hours spent on the road, especially during the longer runs, were a great opportunity to reflect on my life and the Savior's influence on it. After one such extended run, I returned home with a desire to read the book of Job in the Old Testament. As I read Job's declaration, "I know my redeemer liveth" (Job 19:25), I was filled with an over-powering witness that He does indeed live, He knew of my trial and how it would be resolved, and He wanted me to have greater faith in Him while His plan proceeded.

In September I got a call from the hiring manager at Informix, indicating there might be a chance to hire me on. He then asked if I was still interested. "Absolutely," I answered.

"There is still a hiring freeze," he continued, but he informed me that my name had been circulating within the company the past six months as a "critical hire," and they were going to apply for an exception to hire me. I was elated and humbled to find out there might be a position after all. I confess I had so many doubts during that six-month trial—questioning and second-guessing the answers I had received—that I felt a growing shame for my lack of faith as things looked more hopeful.

Even though IBM had acquired Informix, the acquisition wasn't final, so the offer letter read Informix Software, LLC; I was being hired by Informix, just as I had been told I would be. As I look back on that summer, I was certainly blessed, but I realized that I shouldn't have worried and whined so much. Like so many journeys, when you're in the thick of things, you can't often appreciate how far you've come or where you're headed.

Less than two years into my job, then at IBM, I wondered about the several companies I had applied to, and especially about the company I received an offer from that I had turned down. Every company except one had gone under, and that lone company had gone through several rounds of layoffs since I had talked with them. My imperfect patience had paid off.

• • •

As I sorted through the pile of papers on the kitchen table, I saw a packet that I must have received soon after the crash, but had never noticed. It was from the Utah Office of Crime Victim Reparations and described how uncovered expenses could be paid by their program with the funds coming from surcharges and fines levied against criminal offenders. That seemed very just and appropriate, and I contacted them for help. They were hugely instrumental in helping me pay many of the bills. It was an incredible blessing to have our financial issues, incurred because of the crash, paid for in so many miraculous and timely ways. My final out-of-pocket costs to cover the medical and funeral expenses were very minimal after the anonymous community donations (for which I am so grateful) and the victim reparations assistance were factored in. My faith had been tested and strengthened, and we had been given an adequate settlement indeed.

Just as "the Lord blessed the latter end of Job more than his beginning" (Job 42:12), I too felt I would be richly provided for with the types of wealth money can't buy and that the blessings were just beginning to be paid out.

• • •

19

Healing and Hope

One morning as I was studying the Bible, I read the words
"It is not good that the man should be alone" (Genesis 2:18). I
thought of my "man cave" home office downstairs and wondered
why Michelle had never used that line to coax me out of it. As
that sentence rang through my head over and over, I knew that
I wasn't going to be a bachelor for long. Although most bishops
are married—the "husband of one wife" according to qualifica-
tions provided in the book of Timothy in the New Testament
(1 Timothy 3:2)—I was told by my Church leaders after the crash
that there was no precedent for whether or not a widower could
serve as a bishop, and so I was allowed to continue serving as the
bishop. As difficult as it was to continue serving, I think the congregation needed the time to grieve just as I did, without another
significant disruption so soon after the crash.

As the weeks passed, I began to appreciate why Timothy had
indicated a bishop should have a wife. I found that trying to heal,
move forward, be strong for my two sons, serve the congregation

members, and continue to work for my employer, all without the help and assistance of my wife and best friend, was extremely difficult. I desperately missed the support of Michelle. And if I wasn't going to be single for long, I wondered how weird it would be to date a bishop.

My Sundays became the most difficult day of the week to endure. I would tearfully awake very early in the morning and have my personal prayer and gospel study. Then I was off to some early meetings, back home to awaken the boys and get them ready, and then back to church for three hours of worship. Michael would then take Sam home, while I stayed at the church for several hours of appointments with members of the congregation, ministering individually to those needing temporal welfare or spiritual assistance. When my work was completed, I would frequently sit in the bishop's office alone, emotionally exhausted and weeping, so sad that I couldn't feel of Michelle's strength and support upon returning home. And yet as I walked out of the church each Sunday, a sustaining strength would come into my life, giving me the ability to continue to serve another week.

The loneliness was brutal. I endured it as long as I could, but after several months, I decided it was time to go on a few dates. I had yet to connect with any other widowers with children for advice on how to get through this, although I did benefit greatly from the advice of a dear friend who was a single parent with two children. I was curious how much Michelle might be a part of this process too, but I never felt it was a good idea to ask, "Hey, honey, who should I go out with?"

After a few initial dates, I realized I was just trying to replace the companionship I had with Michelle or in some way bring her back. I didn't want to hurt anyone's feelings in the process, but I still needed time to emotionally heal; I couldn't date to replace

Michelle. My identity was so intertwined with hers, and now that we were separated, I was being forced to become reacquainted with Chris Williams.

Michelle was often the voice of reason when I tried to push myself too hard or take on too much. When I was unemployed and training for my first marathon, she helped me stick to a training schedule that helped me complete the race. She was also a voice of reason whenever I was about to do something foolhardy.

A case in point is when I paid seventy-five dollars to race in my sixth marathon, and then I never trained for the race; I had in effect just bought a very expensive race jersey for a race I hadn't prepared for. In my defense, it was an April marathon, and I was just too busy skiing to train. I think I had my priorities straight. Ben and I went the night before the race to pick up the jersey, and I found myself caught up in the excited anticipation of the race with all the other runners. I couldn't resist the energy and excitement accompanying the pre-race activities, so I came home with the race packet and told Michelle I was just going to run the race anyway. Despite her warnings, I started the race. I took a cell phone with me in case I ran into trouble, and I called her at various points on the route. It wasn't my fastest race, but I finished and promised that I wouldn't pay for any more races that I wasn't going to train for.

• • •

Without Michelle's wonderfully moderating influence in my life, I found that I could again make some pretty ill-considered decisions.

Using as inspiration my first marathon that helped me through unemployment, I figured that participating in some sort

Chris and his friends ran the Wasatch Back Relay
in tribute to Chris's family, June 2007

of athletic challenge would help me push through this trial and the accompanying loneliness. I decided to race in a triathlon. My thought processes were something like, *I know how to swim and ride a bike, and certainly how to run; how difficult can it be?* It was, after all, just *a half-mile swim, a twelve-mile bike ride, finishing with a leisurely three-mile jaunt,* I reasoned. So, seven days before the Echo Reservoir Triathlon, I bought a bike, went out for a few rides, took a few laps in a hotel pool on a business trip that week, and went out for a few runs. I drove by myself to the race parking area, put my gear on my back and started to bike toward the starting line and transition area. As I started pedaling while I was messing with my headphones and music player, trying to find a song to get me in the right mindset for the race, I hit a speed bump and crashed. That was nature's first warning that I should take the jersey, turn back, and go home.

Pressing forward, I arrived at the transition area, set up my gear, and entered the water in my short-sleeve waterskiing wet-suit, not realizing that a metal ball and chain would have given me more buoyancy. Within minutes of the start of the race, I began to panic as people thrashed all around me, and I was unable to see much or breathe well in the murky, choppy water.

Perhaps it was the pure adrenaline that propelled me one hundred feet from the shore, but when the sensation of being in a piranha feeding frenzy subsided, I realized I was out of breath, sinking, and feeling as if I were ready to drown. I desperately wanted to raise my hand and be taken from the race, but I couldn't see a kayak anywhere nearby to rescue me. All I could think of as I treaded water were the words "baby steps, baby steps," while I looked for the buoy in the distance that I needed to swim around. My silent prayer was quick and simple: *I'm sorry I'm such an idiot; please get me out of here.* Slowly I made my way forward around the first buoy, then the second, and twenty minutes after the start of the swim, I was exiting the water to the collective exasperation of the ministering angels unfortunately assigned to my care.

It was perhaps one of the craziest things I had ever done. But when I finished the race, I felt a sense of terrific accomplishment—I finished twenty-third of twenty-seven people in my age group—and so I immediately signed up for the next scheduled triathlon in August.

In effect, I was pushing myself way too hard; I was trying to hurry as fast as I could through the grieving, loneliness, and pain, and it was beginning to take a staggering toll. After one very difficult Sunday, and feeling that I couldn't carry on even after "pulling up" and pleading for grace, I received a call from James Wood; he wanted to meet with me. As we talked, he said that the Savior "no longer required this sacrifice" of me and that I was to be released from my stewardship as bishop on August 19. It was a bittersweet day.

I knew I needed to focus on rebuilding my family and seeing that my boys were healing, yet I felt that the blessing to serve
as a bishop was one more thing that I was losing because of the
crash. I had only served for a year and six months while most
bishops serve for five years. During the meeting in which I was
released, the new bishop was announced and asked to come forward and sit on the stand while I approached the pulpit to share
some thoughts. I bore a witness of the Savior and of His love, re-
counting the many experiences I had passed through as evidences
of His ability to teach and heal. As I concluded my remarks, I
turned and saw that the new bishop had rightly taken my seat on
the stand, in between the two counselors, so I exclaimed aloud,
"Hey, that's where I was sitting!" It was all in fun, but it was
shocking to feel that the calling had come and gone so quickly.

Six days later, I competed in the Jordanelle Triathlon. This
time I finished thirteenth of twenty-seven participants in my age
group, an accomplishment which pressed into my thick skull the
truth that a month of training was better than one week.

Before the race, I noticed that a couple who used to live in
my neighborhood, Jason and Amy Zander, were also signed up
to compete. They had moved to West Jordan, Utah. When I saw
them earlier in the summer, they had asked if I was dating, and at
that time I told them I wasn't ready yet. They had wanted to line
me up with a wonderful woman they knew, a competitive triath-
lete named Mikkel Fuhriman Jones. I hadn't given their invitation another thought until I saw their names on the Jordanelle
register. I really enjoyed the challenge of the triathlon but decided
I would prefer a friend to participate in the races with, rather
than competing alone.

I called Amy and told her I was ready to be introduced to
Mikkel. There was a church meeting (an evening devotional)

being held the Sunday evening after the triathlon, and Amy suggested we could all attend it together. I consider myself a spiritual guy, and, of course, I love going to my church meetings, but in hindsight, that was not the best venue for me to meet and get to know someone for the first time. I entered the building waiting for Jason and Amy to arrive, and I noticed a very attractive woman in the foyer who wasn't wearing a wedding ring. For a moment I jokingly thought, *If this Mikkel doesn't work out, maybe I'll ask this woman out on a date.*

Jason met me in the foyer, and we took our seats in the chapel. As I waited for Mikkel to join us, the woman I saw in the foyer walked to the row I was seated on and proceeded to move in to sit by me. I didn't know if I should say "that seat's taken" or just let her sit down. As I watched her come closer, wondering what I should say, Jason leaned toward me and said, "That's Mikkel."

We sat through the meeting, listening to the speakers, unable to say much to each other without being disruptive. Awkwardly, we both took out little notebooks, like we were going to learn something that night. I looked down at what she was writing because the meeting was about strengthening the family. I figured she was probably looking at my notepad too. I wanted to pretend to be disinterested and fall asleep or write a silly to-do list like "shave back hair before the weekend, eat more donuts and less fiber, learn to cook cold cereal"—anything to put both of us at ease. Instead I acted as if I were really listening. Meanwhile, her initial impression of me was that I was too serious. It turns out I should have written the joke list.

After the meeting I drove her home and asked if we could go out on a more traditional date. She agreed, and we went to dinner a few days later and had a most fascinating conversation;

Mikkel and Chris at the Ogden Valley Triathlon

it was as if we had known each other for years and were just getting reacquainted. Her husband, Rusty Jones, had succumbed to bone cancer in 2006, leaving her a widow with two children, a four-year-old boy named Parker and a two-year-old girl, Arli. We talked of the trials we had both been through, and we shared the common thought that those experiences had strengthened us spiritually for the future. We agreed that to appreciate greater heights of joy one had to sometimes pass through the deep valleys of sorrow, enduring tests and trials. Our first marriages hadn't set a limit for us; they hadn't been "as good as it gets," but they had set a firm foundation for our lives that were yet to be built.

I was delighted that I had found a friend to race triathlons with, and Mikkel and I participated in the Ogden Valley Triathlon together in September. Mikkel finished first in her age group and fifth overall, while I placed seventh out of twenty-three in my age group, proving to myself that two months of training is even better than one month. When I told her of my first triathlon experience, I think she thought I was trying to be funny. I left it at that.

As we continued to date, I felt so wonderful and comfortable in her presence. She inspired me to be a better person and encouraged me to continue serving, healing, and moving forward. It wasn't long before we were discussing our thoughts regarding marriage. It seemed right, but I wanted to make sure, so I made it a matter of prayer. When I asked my Heavenly Father if Mikkel was the one I should marry, the Spirit whispered to my mind, "She's a good one." It was such a perfect answer for me to receive. I was subsequently thrilled when Mikkel replied, "Yes, yes, a thousand times yes," when I asked her to marry me, and one month later we were married in the Salt Lake Temple.

• • •

20

An Assurance of People as They Can Be

During our first year of marriage, Mikkel and I moved into a new neighborhood. I had taken a different position at work, and we were both fully immersed in the wonderfully challenging process of blending our families together. It was not as easy as I thought it would be, especially for Michael and Sam. The sleepless nights grieving for my children were replaced by sleepless nights filled with prayerful concern for my two sons. I wondered how they would be able to adapt through so many changes.

The unique struggles and challenges that my sons were having seemed to be getting worse over time. Even though I was now married again, I felt very much like a single parent to Michael, who didn't really feel a part of or associated with this new arrangement. Although I had given him many father's blessings of comfort and peace, one day I felt prompted to ask Michael if he would prepare himself to receive a patriarchal blessing, which is a special blessing modeled after the blessing Jacob of the Old

Testament pronounced on each of his sons. This blessing is given by one who is an ordained patriarch, or evangelist, in our church.

As Michael received that special blessing, I understood how I could be a better father for him. There were future opportunities spoken of in the blessing, sure to happen if he made the right choices. I was given the opportunity to see Michael as he really was and to love him unconditionally, with greater patience than I previously ever had as his father. I realized that each of my children would have incredible stewardships made available to them, and I needed to have much greater patience as they made their way toward realizing their own potential.

This perspective and the accompanying patience began to be applied to all that I met or knew. A few weeks after Michael's blessing, I received a call from a counselor at the juvenile detention facility where Cameron was. She introduced herself as one who had been working with Cameron and wondered if I would be willing to assist her with something she was trying to accomplish with Cameron: helping him empathize and more fully appreciate the impact that the deaths of Michelle, Ben, and Anna had had on the lives of my family. She told me that Cameron had prepared some questions that he would like to ask me and asked if I would be willing to meet with Cameron to answer those questions in person? I agreed, hung up the phone, looked at my new family circumstance, and began tallying the many ways my life had changed since February 2007.

Since the certification hearing, I had regularly included Cameron and his family in my prayers, petitioning that they too would feel of the grace and tender love that I had been blessed with. I had particularly included in my prayers a request that Michelle, Ben, and Anna might be permitted to participate in that process by visiting and working with Cameron while he was in the detention facility, envisioning them as some form of ministering angels to him. As I considered all of us working together on both sides of this earthly life, it helped me feel closer to them, even though I never once directly felt that the request had been granted. I did feel, however, that Cameron was being ministered to, and I had committed to myself that if there was something that I could do to help him, I wanted to do it.

A date was set for the meeting, and I began to mentally prepare myself for the visit. At first I didn't tell anyone else about the request; I wanted to be inspired, and I was concerned that I would get outside suggestions for what I should tell him, some that might not be as helpful in helping me stay true to my earlier commitments. In an effort to organize my thoughts and be prepared with something to say, I started to write down how the crash had impacted my life. I struggled to really capture something that I could share with him and I felt the need, given my inability to express my feelings in writing, to fast and pray for greater inspiration.

I received a renewed sense of peace, but as I drove to the detention facility, I realized I still didn't know what I could say that would help with the counselor's request. I arrived early and sat quietly in my car for one last opportunity to gather my thoughts, but with little success. In some frustration I prayed that I would at least not say or do anything that would hinder or set back the work that my Heavenly Father was accomplishing in Cameron's life and that my words and actions would be in harmony with the heavenly and earthly help I was confident he was receiving.

After checking in at the desk, I entered a small reception area where I awaited the counselor. A large, thick security door opened, and she stepped forward into the waiting area, greeting me warmly and thanking me for being so willing to come and help. As we walked toward the room where I would meet Cameron, my mind was quieted, and I felt a growing sense of considerable peace; I knew that the counselor and I were not walking alone. She quickly turned into a small conference room where Cameron was seated, waiting for us to arrive.

He had changed quite a bit since I had seen him nearly two years earlier in the certification hearings. For one thing, his physical stature was much larger. Should I have chosen to physically attack him, there would have been no contest. However, I walked in smiling, with an extended hand of friendship. It's not that I didn't want to be smiling or displaying a sense of friendship, yet it was as if the actions weren't my own.

We sat down across from each other, and the counselor again explained that Cameron was trying to gain a greater appreciation for his actions and had prepared some questions for me to answer. He unfolded a piece of paper and began to ask about my life since the accident, how it affected me, my sons, and my extended family. He wanted to know more about Ben, Anna, and Michelle and what I could relate to him from their lives, to help him know them and to appreciate who they were. I have tried to recall what I answered to each of the prepared questions, but I can't. I don't know what I said, only that I felt calm as I answered each question as directly and concisely as I could.

When he had finished reading the questions and I had finished giving whatever answers I offered, the counselor then asked Cameron, "Is there anything else that you would like to ask Mr. Williams?"

Cameron then dropped the paper, looked directly into my eyes, and asked, "After all that I've done to your family, how is it that you were able to forgive me?" I'll never forget that look. To me, it appeared he wanted to know if there was to be any hope in his life.

I leaned forward and said, "If there is anything you have seen me do, or heard me say, or have read about me regarding the forgiveness, you should know that it was merely the Savior working through me." It was again my privilege to have a front-row seat, watching the Savior call out for His son to come home and be healed. Cameron too had tremendous blessings, opportunities, and privileges available to him if he made the right choices to claim them. The Spirit that filled that room was profound as it pierced both of our hearts with an eternal truth: We are loved by the pure love of Jesus Christ, and He wants us to fulfill our potential.

I don't recall the rest of the conversation; I felt I had been prompted to say exactly what needed to be said. We arose and embraced, and Cameron again thanked me for coming and speaking with him. The counselor was overcome with tears as she too got up and thanked me for coming. As she and I walked out, she expressed certainty that my visit was going to change Cameron's life. She remarked how incredibly powerful it was and then said what a privilege it was to have been a part of it. I felt that she could have just as easily been talking to someone else about *me* and about the powerful effect this experience would have in changing my life too.

I walked toward my car, starting a silent prayer of gratitude for the opportunity to serve. I had a half-smile on my face as I hoped that Michelle was aware of the meeting and pleased with the behavior of her spouse. As I opened my car door, I heard a voice in my mind, coming from over my right shoulder, saying, "Thank you." I immediately recognized that the expression of gratitude came not from Ben, Michelle, or Anna, but from

Cameron's ancestors, his family, that were indeed working with him from the other side. I sat in my car, closed the door, and just cried. I could feel their concern and love for me, and I also knew that of the many people who were praying for the healing of my family, his family too were regularly adding their faith and pleas for my family to be blessed. Most important, I experienced firsthand, more than I ever had before, the great worth of a soul.

• • •

21

The Ties That Bind

At the end of 2008, we were expecting a baby girl, and the number of changes that our family was going through seemed to be escalating rather than subsiding. When Mikkel and I were dating, we talked about the possibility of having children together. In fact, we were fairly specific in the discussion, both agreeing that we wanted at least two more children. But as I considered diapers, baby food, spit-up, sleepless nights, and every other wonderful aspect of having children and realized I wouldn't exactly be a young father, I was tempted to wonder, *What have I gotten myself into?* I still felt it was the right path for me even though it meant a considerable amount of work. I pressed forward, having faith that the joy more children would bring would be greater than anything else I could choose, and in May 2009, our beautiful Emma Williams was born.

Emma was born into a blended family at a time when the four existing siblings were still struggling to find their place. I knew that she was an incredible addition to our family, but I couldn't yet foresee the miraculous effect her presence would have in our home. That would take some time to more fully appreciate.

Days after her birth, we learned that my dad's cancer had metastasized to other parts of his body. He had been diagnosed with melanoma in January 2007, right before the crash, and after fighting it valiantly for two years, he was rapidly succumbing to that terrible disease as it had aggressively spread to his lungs and bones. While each child in my family needed me in a pressing, unique way, my imperfect efforts to be there for them were complicated by my struggle to also be there for my father during his last days. One particular growth in his spine had rendered him paralyzed from the waist down. What he endured being bedridden was so very humiliating, yet he bore it with strength and fortitude. One evening as we visited, I felt in my heart that if I had anything to say before he passed away, now was the time to say it. I had regularly expressed my love and admiration for him each time we were together, but after receiving that prompting, I had the privilege to express my love for him and say good-bye. He passed away two days later.

My father was laid to rest next to the graves of Michelle, Benjamin, and Anna. As hard as his death was to me and my family, especially my mother, I knew that if I would just stay the course and hold on with faith, all would be well one day. Mikkel was such an incredible source of strength, love, and support throughout that time. She knew the trials and challenges of cancer from having lived with it firsthand with Rusty. I felt so very blessed that I had been privileged to meet and marry her, a sentiment that grows every day we're together.

It's hard for me to attend a funeral and not take some kind of reflective accounting of my life to that point. Something about death seems to make me wonder about the life I'm living. My father's funeral was especially powerful as I reviewed so many experiences and decisions I had made in the previous years. I thought of the decision to "let it go" and how it had empowered me, and of the decision to remarry and have Emma. My mind recollected one event in particular that wasn't a terribly remarkable one, compared to the others, but I recalled it over and over in the days following my father's funeral.

• • •

A few months after the crash, I had had a discussion with two filmmakers, Christopher Clark and Patrick Parker, who wanted to create a documentary on forgiveness. They subsequently filmed me talking about the challenges I would be asked to endure in the future, and how the forgiveness had helped me to meet them and overcome them.

I hadn't heard from them since the initial filming, and so I wondered if the documentary had ever been made. The thought that I needed to contact them continued to press itself into my mind, so I contacted Chris, inquiring how I could see the finished movie. He wrote back and indicated that they never had completed their film as shortly after the interview he and Patrick had begun working for the LDS Church media group producing short, faith-promoting videos called Mormon Messages. We got together for lunch and broached the idea of possibly filming a Mormon Message about forgiveness, perhaps incorporating the interview footage from 2007. We discussed the story's potential to bless the lives of others and thought that early 2010 might be a good time to move forward with it.

As Chris and Patrick refined the format of the message, they realized they wanted Cameron to be a part of the project. Because of the necessary restrictions imposed at the detention facility, none of us could figure out how to finagle it. However, a few days later, I was notified by the parole board that Cameron would be allowed to stay at his home during the final months of his sentence in order to give him the best opportunity to move forward in his life. I explained my desire for him to be part of a Mormon Message and was told that they were fine with it if Cameron wanted to participate. With the opportunity for Cameron and me to both be a part of the message, Chris and Patrick made arrangements to begin the filming. It had been nearly one year since Cameron and I had last spoken with each other. I was anxious to see him again and to express my love and concern for him.

The only scene where Cameron and I needed to be filmed together depicted us meeting at a park bench and speaking with each other. When I saw him that day, I immediately noted that he looked much happier and hopeful than he had a year earlier. I knew he was being healed in a miraculous way, and I was filled with an immense satisfaction of being a witness to the Savior's love in his life. We spoke as brothers for more than an hour as Chris and Patrick filmed us.

I shared with Cameron how my life had changed since we had last met, reciting many of the things I had pondered after the passing of my father. He spoke of what he was currently pursuing in his life with work and schooling; he was also moving forward from that tragic night. I felt such a remarkable sense of peace as we talked; it was the kind of scene that surely brought a smile to our Father in Heaven's face as He watched two of His sons striving to follow the Savior in deed.

So often in my life I've tried to direct or rush the Savior into producing a blessing or the final outcome during a trial. Like so many things of worth, outcomes take time to

Chris and Cameron during the filming of "My Burden Was Made Light"

materialize—sometimes years and years—and when I'm in the thick of the trial, I have the worst perspective on that timing or when it will end. As Cameron and I talked together on the bench, there was one thing I could see that had changed dramatically in the few years since the crash: my patience with the timing of the Savior's plan for me. I found that my patience had increased considerably, fortified by my willingness to endure. I could see that I had been blessed with a greater capability to know that if my prayers weren't being answered in the way I expected, they would be answered in a much better way, and it would be worth the wait.

The Mormon Message was entitled "My Burden Was Made Light," and it was made available for Internet viewing in July 2010. I have read and heard so many stories since of how this video has helped others to let the Savior take their burdens, exchanging them for His yoke. His invitation is as urgently needed by so many today, as it was when he taught, "Come unto me, all ye that labour and are heavy laden, and I will give you rest. Take my yoke upon you, and learn of me; for I am meek and lowly in heart: and ye shall find rest unto your souls" (Matthew 11:28–29).

• • •

Sam and Michael continued to grieve and move forward, but they started to receive a rest to their souls from our beautiful little Emma, who was then one year old. During her entire first year with us, I hadn't been able to see that the answer I sought regarding my family would come through her.

She was cute, as most babies are when they are born, so it was natural to love her, but it was her naturally gregarious, happy personality that emerged as she grew older that provided a tremendous healing influence, softening hearts and bringing us together as one. Because I was trying to endure with patience, perhaps I wasn't looking so carefully for an answer; I was just moving from day to day, knowing that someday it would all work out. Yet at some point I noticed that Michael was home a little more often than he had been and spending more time with the other children than he had previously. As he interacted with us, I saw that his attention was focused on little Emma, and I could see she was enthralled by her big brother Michael.

As Emma grew older, the family grew closer together. She was the glue that was bringing us, and binding us, together as a family. I could see the Savior's hand more clearly in the healing process as well. I better understood the feeling I had had that I wouldn't be single for long so Emma's arrival wouldn't be delayed. I could appreciate the guidance I received that there was someone whom I was going to meet and marry. Our new family wasn't a replacement for the families Mikkel and I had prior to

Emma and Michael as Michael leaves on his mission

the tragedies that took our spouses, nor was Emma a replacement for Ben or Anna. Our family was a sublime addition to the growing family that now spanned both sides of this life, bringing all of us closer together.

We began to establish new, wonderful traditions as a family to draw us even closer together. It wasn't a quick process, but over time hearts were healed, then sealed together as one. Sam's healing and his resiliency and ability to embrace the many changes he has endured has been miraculous. Hearing him talk about the Savior and the expectation he has that he'll someday be with his mother, brother, and sister demonstrates a depth to his character that he could have received in no other way. He has been richly blessed.

Michael too has cultivated a deep and abiding testimony of Jesus Christ as well as the plan of happiness we can all partake of. Desiring to share that with others, he prepared for and accepted a call to serve as a missionary in the Raleigh, North Carolina, area. After dropping him off in Provo, Utah, at the Missionary Training Center, to begin his two years of missionary service, I felt in my heart the great satisfaction and pride that Michelle has for our son. I knew that Michelle has been able to have a profound impact on Michael and Sam because she is an angel, with all the wisdom, power, and perspective that accompanies that station, and I believe that has made all the difference. She knows what her two sons are capable of becoming; it just took some time and patience for me to see it, and it was definitely worth the wait.

Parker and Arli seem to have adapted to our new family arrangement quite well; they love playing with Sam and Emma and writing to Michael on his mission. When I was dating Mikkel, I found out that Mikkel's husband, Rusty, and I have the same pioneer ancestor in our family tree. Parker and Arli are my third cousins twice removed. That may be a bit distant, but it has been a wonderful blessing realizing that they were already a part of my family before they became part of the immediate family. And Emma continues to enthrall and captivate us with her wonderful happy personality and her innate love of life.

And what about that commitment to have at least two children? On February 25, 2012, we welcomed into our family another beautiful baby girl, Caroline Williams. She wasn't due until March 13, but perhaps Michelle, Benjamin, and Anna pulled some strings so she could be born into our family early, on Ben's birthday. Maybe it was their way of reminding us that as the family grows, they're still very much a part of it.

• • •

22

A Fresh Perspective

It's hard to think of an experience I've had that hasn't involved revisiting the lesson that we need to "keep moving forward" in order to get through our trials. One final example stands out in my mind.

In the fall of 2006, Michelle, Michael, and I participated in a youth "Pioneer Trek" outing where we reenacted some of the experiences the Mormon pioneers endured as they walked over one thousand miles from the Midwest to Utah. In preparation for that outing, we researched some of my pioneer ancestors and the challenges and trials they had passed through.

I studied the lives of two of my ancestors, Thomas David Evans and Priscilla Merriman Evans. Thomas had lost his left leg below the knee cap when he was nine, joined The Church of Jesus Christ of Latter-day Saints when he was sixteen, and served four proselytizing missions in Wales, walking thousands of miles on a wooden leg. Priscilla's motto in life was "Don't look back, but onward." They emigrated from Wales by boat to America, took a train to St. Louis from the East Coast, and pushed a hand-cart over one thousand miles from St. Louis across the plains in 1856 as part of the Bunker handcart company. Their lives were an example of literally moving forward, and I owe much of what I am to ancestors like them.

On the last evening of the trek, Michelle was videotaped answering the question, "What do you hope this [Pioneer Trek] does for Michael and his future?"

Michelle replied, "I hope it just teaches him the lesson that they didn't give up, and they carried on even when it was hard, and it wasn't popular." She then went on to explain, "We have a quote from my husband's great-great-grandmother, Priscilla Evans, that talked about people laughing at them as they practiced their beliefs and demonstrated their faith in Jesus Christ." She added, "Rather than worrying about peer pressure and being concerned about what other people might think, stand true and stand strong, and care about what's in [the] heart, and what's good." What a treasure it is to have that recorded witness, encouragement, and admonition from Michelle, and how very true and timely it was.

At the end of the trek reenactment, I felt prompted to write the following in my journal:

After pondering on the experience of my ancestors, I find myself without excuse. When a life of ease or pleasure, or a selfish thought to let someone else do the "heavy lifting" comes to mind, I must be up and doing, and do my duty. I must go forward, enduring all that I'm asked to endure.

In the Rock Creek Hollow Camp on the high plains of Wyoming, through which my ancestors had passed, there is a

Michelle and Chris at Rock Creek Hollow, Wyoming

monument erected in honor of those pioneers, and it has but one word prominently inscribed upon it: "Remember." As I looked at that word and pondered the sacrifice of my ancestors and their dedication to the Savior, I knew that if I would do likewise, I would be better prepared to handle anything that this life could throw at me. In my experience, I have found that you can't always appreciate why you should keep moving forward until you've gone far enough to turn around and see the progress you've made.

• • •

I was raised at the foot of Mt. Olympus. Not *the* Mt. Olympus in Greece. Rather, the Mt. Olympus that overlooks the Salt Lake Valley in Salt Lake City, Utah. Growing up in its shadow, I probably saw that mountain every day of my life without really noticing it. If I did pay any attention to the steep face or the lofty peak, I would dismiss the observation with a thought about climbing it one day. It took twenty-one years of my life at its base before I finally attempted the ascent, and that attempt came at the planning and prodding of a dear friend.

There is a preferred trail to the summit that begins at the western foot of the mountain. We chose instead to hike from the eastern side, through Neff's canyon. This is not much of an improved trail; in fact, toward the summit there is no trail at all. It was bushwhacking and bouldering for most of the 4,500-foot ascent—a long arduous climb. It was steep and fraught with danger; at one point while pulling myself up a ledge, I came face to face with three rattlesnakes quietly enjoying the hot summer sun.

When we arrived at the top, I was awestruck at the view of the valley below—how breathtaking and beautiful it was—and I thought of how it had been there my entire life and I never had fully appreciated it before that day.

• • •

It has been more than five years since the night of the crash. I feel I have travelled forward sufficiently for that experience not to be so painful to revisit or recall. I have a new perspective on the deep and abiding love that I have for Michelle, Ben, and Anna and on how it has grown because of the separation—often penetrating the veil that separates us and strengthening the ties that bind us together eternally. I can better appreciate the great blessing that Mikkel is in my life and how my love for her and Parker and Arli deepens and grows. I continue to be in awe of the binding, healing "glue" Emma is to our family, and I'm confident our little Caroline will add tremendously to that process. My sons have been healed and have both recently noted how their lives have been richly blessed because of what they have endured.

After that fateful night, I found that it was very hard to move forward and cover a substantial amount of distance (as in my training for a marathon). In the first few years after the crash, I

The Williams family in July 2011
Front (left to right): Arli, Emma, Parker. Back: Chris, Mikkel, Michael, Sam

was better off thinking in terms of "baby steps," as I did during one of my triathlons. But within these five years, exercising patience with my progress, it has become progressively easier for me to keep moving forward. The grieving and longing for my family hasn't stopped, nor do I expect it to until we're together again, but those moments of pain are increasingly sweet and positive experiences.

As I continue to ponder the personal growth that has come from losing half of my family in a tragic crash, and from every other trial or tribulation through which I have journeyed, I can now see that much of what I've experienced has enabled Chris Williams to learn something about Chris Williams, and there was no other way I could have learned these things about myself. I think we must be taught, tested, and tried, or we'll never come to know what we are really made of, and we won't be prepared to one day see ourselves as we are seen in heaven.

The word "repentance" in the New Testament is translated from the Greek word *metanoia*, which means "a change of mind." Repentance can bring about a new view of God, about oneself, and about the world. Trials and tests become an invitation to see things as God sees them and to change our thoughts and actions to live according to the way things really are—they are an invitation to repent! Perhaps one of the reasons the trials in my life were allowed to occur was to strengthen my faith and assurance in the person I could become, the person that my Father in Heaven already knew that I could be.

We bind ourselves together in this life through love. When our marriage and family unions are established by one who is authorized to act on behalf of our Heavenly Father, we can be bound together eternally through love. We're placed into circumstances and associations on this earth, and we're allowed to have trials and tribulations that we may strive and desire to become a united people one day in heaven, and our hearts and minds are bound together forever by the pure love of Christ.

One of my favorite Christian hymns, "Come Thou Fount of Every Blessing," teaches this binding concept so beautifully:

O to grace how great a debtor,
Daily I'm constrained to be!
Let Thy goodness, like a fetter
Bind my wandering heart to Thee.
Prone to wander, Lord, I feel it,
Prone to leave the God I love;
Here's my heart, O take and seal it,
Seal it for Thy courts above.

(Lyrics by Robert Robinson, hymn in public domain)

My family is being bound to the lives of Cameron and his family by love. It is my constant prayer and faith that one day both families will rejoice with the Savior, together, equally petitioning for His mercy and praising His willingness to suffer, die, and be resurrected so that we could live. Half of my family was taken from this life, and as we have given that incredible burden to the Lord, He has run to us with healing in His wings. What a wondrous miracle it has been my blessing to behold.

Since the crash, I've had many conversations with people searching for peace and forgiveness in their lives, earnestly desiring to know how I was able to let it go and rely wholly on the Savior's grace in my life. I would hope they now understand what I mean when I begin by explaining to them that "I am nothing." It's a frank and honest self-admission to make, to be sure. Who wouldn't want to protect people from seeing you as you really are, a "nobody," unworthy of any adulation whatsoever? But I want people to know what I have learned about myself after experiencing the trials and blessings of my life thus far. For me it is a great key to enduring and moving forward in spite of my many weaknesses and challenges; I am most empowered by the grace of Jesus Christ when I live my conviction that I am nothing and am "less than the least of all saints" (Ephesians 3:8).

We have an advocate who has been given the power and authority to carry all of our burdens, and yet I have met so many people looking and praying for the strength to carry their own burdens. Mine is yet another story of the enabling, healing, and enlightening power of Jesus Christ. He is everything, and I am nothing, and yet "I can do all things through Christ which strengtheneth me" (Philippians 4:13).

I am so grateful for the Savior. I know He lives! The way has been prepared for all to return to our eternal home if we will desire it. This is my experience with forgiveness, letting go, moving forward, and being healed.

What burden could you lay at the Lord's feet, *today*, that He might be allowed to work miracles in your life?